How to Start Living the RV Life on a Tight Budget

A Budget Friendly RV Lifestyle Startup Guide

By

Robert Nichols

Copyright © 2018 – **Valley Of Joy Publishing Press**

All Rights Reserved.

No part of this publication may be reproduced, stored in a retrieval system or transmitted in any form or by any means, electronic, mechanical, photocopying, recording or otherwise without the proper written consent of the copyright holder, except brief quotations used in a review.

Published by:

Valley Of Joy Publishing Press

Cover & Interior designed

By

Jessica Roberts

First Edition

CONTENT AT A GLANCE

Foreword 8
Benefits of RV Living 10
   Is Living In an RV or Van Right For Me? 11
   Setting Up a Cost Comparison 13
      How Much You Can Save 17
      What to Consider 18
   Preparing for RV Living 19
      Create a Plan for Living on the Road 19
Downsizing for RV Life 21
   Getting Rid of Things 22
Choosing The Right RV 25
   Types of Recreational Vehicles 26
      Fold-Down Campers 26
      Hybrid Trailers 28
      Pull Trailers 29
      Truck Campers 30
      Van Conversions 31
      Motorhomes 32
      Toterhomes and Toy Haulers 35
   Where to Find Used RV's to Buy 36
   9 Things to Consider When Choosing an RV or Van 37
      Cost 37
      Driving Skills 40
      Mechanical Skills 41

- Licensing 41
- Vehicle Use 42
- Level of Comfort 42
- Cost of Living 43
- Necessary Utilities 44
- Tow Vehicles 44

How to Protect Your RV 47
- Regular Inspections 47
- Lots of Caulk 50
- Update and Maintain Batteries 51
- Update and Inspect Smoke and Gas Detectors 51
- Replace or Clean Filters 52
- Monitor Fluid Levels 52
- Servicing Engines and Generators 53
- Maintenance and Cleaning of Holding Tanks 53
- Sanitize and Clean Drains, Faucets and Shower Heads 54
- Maintaining Good Tire Care 54
- Check Appliances 55
- Maintain Detail 55
- Lubricate the Seals of Slide Outs 56

The Ideal RV Toolkit 58
- The Right Small Tools 58
- The Right Kind of Air Compressor 60
- A Reliable Tire Gauge 61
- Two Sets of Wheel Chocks 62
- Additional Safety Features you can Add 63

Utilities in an RV 66

- How the Plumbing Works 67
- Utility Hookups 68
- A Self Contained Unit 68
- Utility Sources 69
- Protecting and Purifying Water in an RV 70
- Communications on the Road 74
  - Mail 74
  - Telephone 76
  - Internet 76
  - Banking 78
  - Television 78
- Living on the Road 80
  - Where to Stay Rent Free 80
    - Business Lots 80
    - Small Town Venues 82
    - Free Campgrounds 84
    - Dry Camping 84
    - Staying at Casinos 85
    - Exchanging Work for Living 85
    - Volunteering 86
    - Finding Free Rent Deals 87
    - Why Some Charge More 88
    - Finding Reasonably Priced Parks 89
- Safety while Living on the Road 91
  - Defensive Driving 92
  - Vehicle Upkeep 92
  - Safe Camping Techniques 93

- Prepare for Issues 95
- Have an Escape Plan 95
- Fire Safety 96

Heating and Cooling in a Vehicle 103
- Reflectix 104

Food and Staying Healthy 113
- Stocking Food 113
- Food Preparation 116
- Cooking Methods on the Road 117
- Staying Healthy and Clean 118
- Health Care on the Road 121

Finding Entertainment & Making Money On the road 123
- Finding Cheap Entertainment 123
- Making Money while you Travel 125

RV Maintenance and Upkeep 128
- Winterizing Your RV 129
  - Winterizing the Water System 129
  - Winterizing the Chassis 131
  - Winterizing the Interior 131
- RV Tire Safety and Maintenance 132
- Dumping and Cleaning the Sewer Tank 134
  - Personal Protection 134
  - Emptying the Tanks 135
  - Deep Cleaning 136
  - Enzyme Treatments 138
- Cleaning and Sanitizing Your RV 139
  - Dusting and Vacuuming 140

- Windows, Mirrors and Window Treatments 140
- Dashboards and Upholstery 141
- Cleaning the Toilet... 141
- Cleaning the Bathroom.. 143
- Cleaning the Floors 144
- Proper Loading and Packing 145
  - The Importance of Packing and Loading Properly 145
  - How to Balance a Load 146
  - Tips for Packing 147
  - RV Food Storage 148
  - Protecting Your Food... 150
- Last Words.. 153
- Helpful Links & Resources 154

FOREWORD

We started our RV life in 2012, as I took an early forced retirement due to downsizing. As an accountant, I kept crunching numbers to figure out how we would survive in the long run with the house note and all other expenses that we had. The one day a friend told me about RV life. I was not interested at first, didn't think much of that idea. But then I started reading about it, and the more I read more appealing it became.

Again as a number guy, I crunched the numbers and found out we could actually do this and save money. Yes, you heard me right. It would cost us less to live and travel around in an RV than to live in our 20-year-old house. I shared my calculation in this book; you can take a look and compare your own numbers and see how your numbers would look.

This book is a compilation of all the things a person should consider when choosing to go with the RV lifestyle. But the important part of this life is saving money, as I said, by going with RV life, we are now saving money and you can too, as long as you do it the right way. I share my ideas, experience, and thoughts about how to start an RV life, safely, while enjoying the beautiful outdoors and finally be able to live the life we once dreamed of.

For some, the idea of full time living in an RV or van may seem like a crazy option. Who would suddenly decide to give up everything and go on the road with the intention of traveling full time or living off the grid. While it is true this lifestyle isn't for everyone; it can be a wonderful lifestyle for some.

In this book, I am going to consider the benefits you can enjoy from full-time RV or van living, how you can start the process and how you can do it for free or cheap. All of the information can be applied to RV or van living, but in this book, I will refer to both as RV for simplicity. Let's start by looking at the benefits of RV living.

BENEFITS OF RV LIVING

There are many reasons why people choose to live full time from an RV. Let's consider the benefits and see which ones appeal to you. Living an RV lifestyle comes with less stress: there is no property or home to take care of, no property taxes to pay and not a lot of stuff to stress over or maintain.

In addition, there is less stress because you are able to have more time for the activities you enjoy. When you live on the road, you won't have many time commitments beyond those you choose to make. Imagine what life is like when you can simply wake up in the morning and spend the day doing what you want to do.

Perhaps the biggest reason many choose to live in an RV is the chance to travel and see everything our great country has to offer. You can simply move on when you have seen everything you want to see and travel to another location where you can see and explore more of the country. You'll also be able to travel with the weather so you can be warm in the winter and cool in the summer.

You can travel to all the areas you've read about and dreamed of going.

Another reason many are choosing to live the RV lifestyle is the reduced cost of living. While you can have high end living in an RV, most choose to live a modest lifestyle in an RV. Starting out with a cheap RV, staying in cheap or free locations and living on a budget can certainly allow you to have a reduced cost of living.

Then there is the fact that you won't buy as much since you won't have anywhere to fit it in an RV. Based on these benefits you may think that RV living is a good idea for you. But is living in an RV right for you? Let's see what you need to consider.

IS LIVING IN AN RV OR VAN RIGHT FOR ME?

If you have an RV or van you have the option of living in a way that separates you from the cost of everyday living. However, you need to make sure RV living is right for you. Let's take a moment to make sure that RV living is right for you.

Are you at a point in your life where you're tired of the process of everyday living? Is your cost of living expenses getting too high to handle? Do you prefer spending your time in nature rather than in traffic? Do you often feel like walking away from it all? Often the best answer to these questions is RV living on the road or living off the grid (to a degree), and it can come with a number of benefits.

However, this option isn't for everyone. Adapting a vehicle to your personal needs is something that requires a little bit of creativity and lot of hardiness. In some situations, it can be an uncomfortable and difficult process to get used to at first. If living in an RV sounds useful to you, there are three main questions you need to ask yourself:

1. Are you willing to live away from stores, hospitals, and doctors?
2. Are you willing to live with limited modern plumbing?
3. Do you like being alone and not easily connecting with others?

While you may find yourself answering no to at least one of these questions, consider whether or not you can adjust to an alternative living situation. You should also take the time to consider how you can save money living in an RV and whether or not you can make the necessary sacrifices to save money living on the road.

Moving into an RV full time can certainly save you money, but on the other hand, it can also be a costly expense if it doesn't work out for you. Often it depends on your circumstances and the choices you make. Let's take a look at how you can save money in an RV and what you need to do to make the lifestyle work for you.

SETTING UP A COST COMPARISON

The best way to determine if living in an RV is beneficial to you is to do a comparison of your potential financial benefits. Let see how you can set up a comparison.

The first thing you need to do is make a list of all your current expenses such as the following:

- Rent or mortgage
- Utilities

- Repair and maintenance
- Insurance and taxes
- Food
- Clothing
- Gas
- Social Expenses
- Any other regular expenses

Next, you want to make a second list of expenses. Include all the expenses from above that you plan to have continued when you live out of an RV and eliminate those expenses won't have anymore. Then add in any new expenses such as the following:

- Camping fees
- Repairs and upkeep
- Utilities
- Vehicle payments
- Fuel cost

Now subtract the total of the first list from the total of the second list to see if living on the road out of an RV will save you any money. If you find the opposite is true then perhaps staying where you are is the better option. But if you are going to be able to save money in an RV then let's keep reading.

My Monthly expenses (While we lived at home)

Items	Expenses
Rent/Mortgage	$1,550
Utilities	$525
Repair & Maintenance	$250
Tax & Insurance	$625
Food & Clothing for two	$650
Health Insurance for two	$750
Credit Card Payments	$450
Car Payment & Fuel cost (Two Cars)	$1150
Social & Other expenses	$375
Total	**$6,325**

This is how our monthly budget looks now (RV living)

Items	Expenses
Camping fees	$400
Repairs & Upkeep	$250
RV payment & Insurance	$775
Fuel Cost	$600
Health Insurance	$750
Food & Clothing	$650
All other misc. Expenses	$300
Total:	**$2,975**

As you can see in our case, we didn't sacrifice much, but the savings came out to be almost half. Instead of having two cars, we sold the one that we had a bank loan on and kept the older paid off one. So, no more car payment and we paid off our three credit cards when we sold our home. We bought a good used RV where our payment including insurance came to about $775/month.

We had a good bit of equity in your home, so when we sold it, after paying off the credit cards we were still able to make a sizeable retirement investment, and with the rise of the recent stock market, our little retirement investment grew by 27% in just year and a half. We also sold all our furniture, lawn and garden equipment and my

Kawasaki bike and put that money towards the down payment of the RV.

HOW MUCH YOU CAN SAVE

The above cost comparison is just an overview. There is a lot of variables to consider when it comes to how much you'll save by changing to an RV lifestyle. Often the biggest variable is yourself since the decisions you make it going to be a big determining factor in the changes that will have an impact on your finances.

For example, if you purchase an expensive RV at a high-interest rate and always park in fancy resort campgrounds; you may find yourself easily paying as much as you are living in a house. However, if you are willing to start small with a reasonably priced RV and can buy it with cash while locating cheap or free-living options, you can often save a lot of money living from an RV.

If your goal is to save money living from an RV, then you need to be realistic and stick to the basics with simple decisions in order to be successful. Consider the following to see if you would be able to live more frugally.

WHAT TO CONSIDER

In order to live frugally in an RV you'll need to do the following:

- Buy an RV that suits your basic needs
- Know how to do basic repairs to maintain your RV
- Finding a cheap or free place to stay
- Purchasing cheap vehicle insurance
- Practice safe driving habits
- Being close to shopping and services

As with traditional living, it is important to know how costs can affect you. For example, while a campground further from town is cheaper the gasoline costs of traveling into town can actually be more expensive. This is why you need to carefully consider all aspects before deciding if RV living is right for you.

If you decide you want to start RV living, then you can start on the next step in the process, preparing for RV living and choosing an RV that meets your needs.

PREPARING FOR RV LIVING

The first step in preparing for RV living is to give it a try and see if you like it. To do this take the following steps:

- Rent or borrow an RV for a short trip
- Visit a local RV repair shop to learn about typical problems with RVs
- Read about living in an RV from online forums
- Visit campgrounds to get a feel for living in them

Once you've confirmed that RV living is something you are ready to try full time you can start your preparation to transition to full-time RV living. Start by putting a plan in place.

CREATE A PLAN FOR LIVING ON THE ROAD

Leaving your life behind and moving into an RV full time requires a lot of advanced planning since there are going to be a lot of things you'll have to deal with such as:

- The costs of transitioning to RV living
- Choosing the right RV to purchase
- Planning where and how you'll live

- How you'll handle utilities
- How you'll downsize your possessions

The best way to handle all this is to make a list of any issues you think you'll face, prioritize those issues and then come up with a plan for how to deal with each one. Don't expect to have answers right away as many of these situations will require extensive planning.

The next step in the process to prepare yourself for RV living is to downsize your possessions. Let's look at how you can simplify your life to prepare for living in a small RV on the road.

DOWNSIZING FOR RV LIFE

Obviously, the biggest downside to RV living is the space limitation. There's a big difference between a house of 1,000 to 3,000 square feet and an RV with 300 to 400 square feet or even less if you choose to live out of a converted van. When it comes to your possessions you need to choose one of six options:

1. Sell
2. Keep
3. Minimize
4. Trade
5. Give Away
6. Store

No matter what you choose, remember that once you get rid of something you can't get it back. Also keep in mind that if you choose to store something, it can get ruined if stored for too long. Storing items will make it easier to restart your life if RV living doesn't work out for you.

On the other hand, choosing to sell items you no longer need can help get you the money needed to buy a vehicle to live out of and have some money on hand for a while.

The one factor that is sure, getting rid of excess things is the hardest thing you'll do. It can be a very overwhelming task. It is best to start this process as soon as possible since you'll want to do it slowly and correctly. The more time you have to decide on sentimental items the better.

For some, the process is easier than others. The first step is to go around your house and get rid of anything that isn't necessary for your everyday life or has an emotional attachment. For others, the process can be more difficult, especially if you've formed an emotional attachment to your items or already have a minimalist approach to your possessions.

GETTING RID OF THINGS

Once you are ready to start getting rid of things, there is a process to follow. Start by dividing your things into piles and put them in boxes. Divide everything into eight different categories:

1. Give to family and friends
2. Sell on eBay
3. Sell in a garage sale
4. Sell on Craigslist
5. Donate to a thrift store
6. Sentimental items to keep
7. Items necessary for everyday life
8. Items to throw away

This process is going to get your house really messy, real fast. If possible try to take a box with you whenever you leave the house to either dispose of or take somewhere. Schedule a garage sale as soon as possible to get rid of things. While getting money to save is helpful, it is also just as important to get rid of the items and get them out of your life.

Start posting ads on Craigslist and eBay right away and keep them going. The goal is to get results right away so you can have more room to sort through and get rid of items. Hopefully, as your house starts looking emptier, it will give you more motivation to get rid of items, even those with a hard decision.

After a while you'll find yourself down to the items that you are sentimentally attached to or those that are necessary to everyday living. At this point, you likely won't be able to get rid of anymore. Often times this is still going to be twice as much as you can fit in an RV or van. So you'll still need to go through things a second time and get rid of more.

As you keep going, the decision to get rid of things is going to get harder. You may even find you need to give up a hobby in order to find room. For some, the process is especially hard if they are the sentimental type and easily for attachments.

Now you can move on to the major step in the process, choosing the right RV or vehicle for life on the road.

CHOOSING THE RIGHT RV

Class A and C Motorhomes   **Fifth Wheels**   **Toy Haulers**

Van Campers and Class Bs   **Travel Trailers**   **Hybrids**

It may not seem like a difficult process to find an RV or van that meets your personal and financial needs, but there is actually a lot you need to consider. After all, you are going to be purchasing a vehicle that will be your house, and you need to take the necessary time and effort to make sure you are making the right decision. There are three things to keep in mind when making your RV purchase:

1. Choose something that is user-friendly with a comfortable floor plan
2. Choose something that meets your lifestyle needs
3. Correctly match a tow vehicle to the vehicle you choose if needed

There are plenty of RV and van options out there, so you are sure to find one that meets your situation, taste, and budget. No matter what vehicle you choose they all have the same basic amenities:

- ☐ Sleeping quarter
- ☐ Living and dining area
- ☐ Galley or kitchen area
- ☐ Plumbing and electrical systems

Pretty much any unit you choose is going to provide you with the basics you need to live. What you need to choose is a unit that works best for you and can be turned into a home that you are willing to live in a while on the road. Let's consider the different types of vehicle options available to you so you can see all your choices and make an appropriate decision.

TYPES OF RECREATIONAL VEHICLES

FOLD-DOWN CAMPERS

Also known as fold-up or pop-up campers, these come in a variety of sizes. They feature canvas sides that fold down into a closed box. The top and lower sides are solid to protect from water damage. For a small use, they can be very spacious, are easy to store when needed, are easy to tow and offer a range of amenities.

The downside is that they can be labor-intensive to take down and setup as well as becoming uncomfortable in wet weather. They are also not permitted in certain camping areas because they don't protect against wild bears.

HYBRID TRAILERS

These offer a combination of a small pull trailer along with a fold-down camper. Some of these designs have canvas sides that pull out for more space while others are a simple hard sided trailer with a roof that drops down when towing. A good example of this type of RV is the Hi-Lo Trailer.

PULL TRAILERS

These offer a great range in size from extremely small to very large, but they also vary greatly in price. The famous teardrop trailers are very small, have little weight and limited amenities. Often these trailers can be towed by small cars and even motorcycles. A regular pull trailer attaches to the rear of a vehicle equipped with a Reese hitch and can be towed by a variety of vehicles.

Fifth wheel trailers are the next size and require a special type of hitch that is located in the bed of a pickup truck, meaning only a pickup is able to tow these trailers. Larger fifth wheel trailers have very spacious living areas and a number of nice amenities that make for a secure and comfortable life on the road.

They can also be left in campgrounds or other areas while the tow vehicle is used to travel around the area. However, some of the larger models will require heavy duty tow vehicles and can be a challenge to park and drive for those who aren't used to driving them; especially in unfavorable weather or road conditions.

TRUCK CAMPERS

These often fit within the bed of a pickup truck. They often have small living quarters, but will give you the basic amenities you need to live. Often they are cheap to buy but do require a heavy duty truck which can be more costly. These units are also more dangerous since they are top heavy and can roll over easily.

VAN CONVERSIONS

This includes all those vans that have high ceilings and can be converted to include utilities and appliances so they can be used as a recreational vehicle. These are easy to drive and are often solidly built. However, they don't have a spacious living area and can sometimes be costly to build and repair.

MOTORHOMES

(Class A Motorhome)

Motorhomes come in four types: A, B, B+, and C.

A Class A motorhome can be built on a truck or commercial bus chassis. You can power them with either a gas or diesel engine and vary in size up to 45 feet in length. They feature high ceilings and are often loaded with a range of amenities.

Class B motorhomes are converted vans with high ceilings and a basic, but small living area.

(Class B Motorhome)

Class B+ motorhomes are a hybrid between Class B and C motorhomes. They are built on a truck or van chassis and are a little bigger than a van conversion with more living space.

Lastly, a Class C motorhome is a unit with a driving area that has over cab beds or cabinets. They are built on a truck chassis with a van based cab section. They can range in size from small to extremely large. There are also a few that are built as toy haulers which we'll discuss soon. A Class C motorhome is wider and higher than

Class B motorhomes, often have more amenities and often come with a large living area.

(Class C Motorhome)

Class A, B+ and C motorhomes typically have slide-out rooms and amenities that most other recreational vehicles don't have such as full-size refrigerators and generators for power. You can easily tow a vehicle with these options so you can explore the area around you without having to drive your home everywhere.

The downside is that these recreational vehicles are costly to buy and maintain, can be difficult to drive and park without special driving skills that not everyone has.

TOTERHOMES AND TOY HAULERS

These are special types of motorhomes and trailers. They are built with a commercial truck engine and are built specially for hauling heavy loads. They often have part living area and part garage with a rear drop down the ramp to store motorcycles or ATVs.

Based on these types consider the following based on your needs:

- For gas mileage and stealth consider a minivan.
- For room and stealth consider a full-size van.
- For comfort and stealth consider a high-top conversion van.

- For comfort consider a Class B RV or a full-size RV.
- For lots of room consider a box van or step-van.
- For backcountry travel consider a pickup with a camper.

Now that you know what types of recreational vehicles exist there are a few questions you need to answer to make sure you are buying something that meets your needs. Buying a recreational vehicle to live in is a physical and financial commitment you want to get right. Consider the following questions and your answers to help you choose the right vehicle for your needs.

WHERE TO FIND USED RV'S TO BUY

If I were you, I would start my search on the internet. But first I would visit a few RV dealers near me and look at all various types of RV's and then try to decide which one of these is right for you. Once you know the type, your search should begin on the net.

Places you can search on the net.

www.eBay.com

www.Craigslist.com

www.RVTraders.com

www.CampingWorld.com/RVSales

You can also look through your local newspaper "for sale" Ads. But before you make an offer on any of these rigs, it is best to check the market value of one of this, just like we do for cars.

To check the current value of an RV, you can visit

http://www.nadaguides.com/RVs

https://rvshare.com/blog/rv-values/

https://www.pplmotorhomes.com/kelley-blue-book-rv

9 THINGS TO CONSIDER WHEN CHOOSING AN RV OR VAN

COST

The cost of a recreational vehicle can vary greatly, so you need to determine what you will pay and how much you want to get for what you are paying. You also want to keep in mind the additional and often hidden costs involved in owning a recreational vehicle that goes beyond the initial purchase cost, sales tax, and registration fees. Keep in mind the cost of the following:

- Repairs
- Maintenance
- Gas
- Camping fees

While you can find ways to reduce some of these costs, you are always going to have these costs to deal with and depending on where you are, and what you need to have done they can be quite high. So make sure you are financially prepared for these potential costs.

Another thing you want to consider is how you will be paying for your RV. People pay for their recreational vehicles in one of three ways:

1. Equity from home or sale of a home.
2. Borrowing from a bank or credit union.
3. Using an RV dealership financing services.

The smartest choice would obviously be to sell your current home and buy an RV outright in cash. Otherwise, you'll have to be prepared to pay interest and fees as you make monthly payments on your loan. This can be costly, especially if you plan to live out of your RV to reduce the cost of living.

As before, when choosing an RV, you want to consider the cost of maintenance and repair. These costs can vary, but in general, labor is about $129 per hour if someone else is making the repairs. The price of parts will often depend on the seller.

Another cost to consider is insurance. This price will be influenced by the age of your RV, the purchase price, and other considerations; the same as when you insure a car. If you keep a vehicle for driving around while your RV is parked, then you may be able to add the RV onto the vehicle policy for a reduced amount.

For example, most older motorhomes won't have a cost over $600 a year. As with your car, it pays to comparison shop until you find an insurance plan that you can afford and one that gives you adequate coverage.

DRIVING SKILLS

Depending on the recreational vehicle you choose, they can be more difficult to drive than a car. So before deciding on which vehicle to purchase you'll want to evaluate your driving skills. Ask yourself two important questions:

1. Are you prepared to drive a large and heavy vehicle on potentially crowded roadways in bad weather?
2. Are you willing to take an RV driving course?

Buying an RV if you've never driven a vehicle of its size and weight can be risky. However, you can learn to drive an RV and with time do well; but you should take the time to master this before you buy an RV.

One good to master this skill is enrolling yourself in an RV driving course in your area. Ask any of the RV dealerships, and they can direct you to one of these courses. But remember a course such as this can set you back around $400-$500, but in my opinion that is a good investment.

MECHANICAL SKILLS

Another thing to consider is your mechanical skills. Most people rely on warranties to protect them if things go wrong when traveling, but help may not always be available.

Depending on where you choose to live in your RV there may be no repair facilities nearby. At the very least, you need to be able to recognize problems when they start to occur. Three basic mechanical skills you should learn before purchasing an RV are:

1. Checking oil levels in generators and engines
2. Knowing when to dump sewer tanks
3. Checking air pressure in tires

LICENSING

To drive a motorhome you typically do not require to have any special license. Generally speaking, if your motorhome is less than 40 feet long and weighs less than 26,000 pounds (gross weight), then you do not need to have any special license to drive it around the country. For more information or to check if your state requires it, here is a link you can visit for more up-to-date information.

https://www.outdoorsy.com/blog/guide-rv-drivers-licenses-requirements

VEHICLE USE

You also want to figure out how you plan to use your RV. You already know you plan to live out of it, but how much. Is it going to be a place where you spend the majority of your time or are you going to just use it as a place to eat and sleep while you spend time outdoors?

Do you plan to work from your RV or go out and find work in the location you spend your time? How you plan to use your RV is going to have a big impact on the type of vehicle you choose to purchase.

LEVEL OF COMFORT

Consider what things you would need to have a comfortable living environment. Do you need a larger shower, a bigger eating area, a larger bed? If you need any of these things, then be sure to find an RV that meets your physical needs when purchasing. Never cut corners when it comes to comfort, that is a sure way to become miserable when trying to live out of your RV.

COST OF LIVING

One thing you definitely want to consider is how much traveling and living you plan to do. Are you going to move to a new destination every couple of months or so? Do you plan to live an entire season in one area before moving? If you plan to drive around a lot to other areas then be sure to consider a recreational vehicle with good gas mileage. Depending on the type of RV you choose you can plan on getting about six to twelve miles per gallon.

On the other hand, if you plan to stay in one place for a longer period of time, then you want to consider the cost of camping. There are plenty of free options, but certain areas can also cost upwards of hundreds of dollars a night depending on where you choose to stay. We'll discuss this more later.

NECESSARY UTILITIES

This is an area where you can cut a few corners and save little extra money. Most people rely on their cell phones to connect to the internet, but if you don't have a cell phone or if you want to cut the cost of paying for a cell phone plan then you can consider using the internet services at public libraries, some businesses and at most campgrounds.

Just keep in mind that most free Wi-Fi connections aren't secure and you may want to pay for your connection in order to ensure privacy; especially if you plan to work from your RV.

TOW VEHICLES

As we discussed before smaller recreational vehicle options such as van and truck campers aren't going to need a tow vehicle while travel trailers are going to require one. If you choose a motorhome, you may want to tow a car since it does give you the flexibility to travel while in an area or in the event of an emergency.

If you choose not to tow an extra vehicle, you might find yourself limited in exploration options while traveling.

If you are set to tow a vehicle, then carefully consider what you want to town, if they are front-wheel or rear-wheel drive, as each of these types are towed very differently. Now if your vehicle is a four wheel or all-wheel drive that you must tow it in a flat dolly where all four wheels are on the dolly and not on the road.

Most common vehicles most RV owners tow (that I have seen) are Toyota Prius, Honda CRV or Toyota Rav4 or something similar. But do make sure these mini SUV's are not all or 4 wheel drive vehicles.

As you can see, choosing a recreational vehicle to live out of isn't the easiest process. However, once you've settled on a choice and made your purchase; there are still a few more steps you need to take before you're ready to head out on the road with your RV. The first step is to learn how you can protect your RV.

Here are two You Tube videos, you must see before buying.

This first one is about what to look for in an RV, it has some good buying tips.

https://www.youtube.com/watch?v=iCo0TGM-WFQ

But this second one is one of those most watched videos where it talks about what to look for when buying a used RV, you should see this to avoid ending up with a lemon.

https://www.youtube.com/watch?v=xx0SPexRHgo

HOW TO PROTECT YOUR RV

The key to having an RV in top condition is to watch for problems and get them repaired as soon as possible. If you don't keep up on this, then issues can become quite expensive, dangerous and potentially undermine your living experience.

Getting in the habit of taking care of these maintenance tasks will be well worth your efforts and lead to good benefits. Let's take a look at thirteen things you need to do to maintain and protect your home on the road.

REGULAR INSPECTIONS

Perhaps the most important thing is to regularly inspect your RV no matter where you're at. Walk in and around your RV, climb up on the roof and check underneath the chassis on a regular basis to look for any problems that need your attention. This will help you discover issues and deal with them promptly before they get worse.

The first step is to walk around the exterior, roof, and underside. There are nine areas to inspect and look for issues:

1. Crawl under your RV and check the chassis for rust. If you notice a large amount of rust, this means that your RV has been exposed to salt or water and has a corroded chassis.
2. Climb up to the roof and make sure it is clean, dry and free of cracks or peeling.
3. Check the engine and generator compartments and make sure they are clean with no signs of corrosion, oil leaks or rust.
4. Inspect windows for fogging and replace any windows that fog.
5. Make sure all jacks and antennas move smoothly.
6. Ensure all steps are working well.
7. Look for any flaws in the body of the RV such as scrapes, dents, bubbling, faded paint or peeling.
8. Ensure the tires are safe, we'll look at that in a later section of this book.
9. Lastly, inspect the slide rooms for any leakage and ensure they work smoothly and easily. Make sure

the rooms have enough support and are spaced correctly for carrying the load.

The second step is to check the inside of your RV or camper. When checking the inside of the RV look for the following:

- Windshield cracks.
- Slide rooms that don't function or sit properly.
- Seats that don't recline properly.
- Windows that don't open and close easily.
- Light fixtures with rust or missing parts.
- Ceiling vents that don't work.
- Televisions or antennas that don't work.
- Damaged or badly stained flooring.
- Air conditioning leaks.
- Faucet leaks.
- Water damage, particularly inside closets and cabinets.
- Cabinet drawers and/or doors that don't easily open and firmly shut.
- Cabinetry parts that need to be replaced.
- Ammonia odor in the refrigerator.
- Rust or dirt under the stovetop burner.

- ☐ Burns, cracks or scratches on the counters.
- ☐ Worn or damaged upholstery.
- ☐ Unpleasant Odors.
- ☐ Propane odors.
- ☐ Mildew smell.
- ☐ Sewer tank smell.

Noticing some of these flaws can be an easy repair, but others can be serious and require major repairs. After you've done your inspection, there are twelve other areas to work on to properly maintain and protect your RV.

LOTS OF CAULK

One of the best ways to protect your RV is to use caulk at any point where water can possibly enter. It doesn't take long to use a caulk gun to spread around your RV. Some areas to caulk include sinks, tubs, exterior lights, windows, awning attachments, air conditioning units, and vents.

Water has a way of sneaking into the smallest of openings and can quickly create a major problem such as mold. So keep the caulking in good order on your RV to help protect against water damage.

UPDATE AND MAINTAIN BATTERIES

A lot of equipment in your RV runs on batteries. This is why you want to update and maintain your batteries regularly. It is important that you keep note of the dates that batteries are installed and keep an eye on how they function and how well they work. If the lights start to dim or have problems then you need to look at the water levels, if they are okay, then you need to consider getting new batteries.

However, not all batteries require water so make sure you know what type of batteries your RV has. Batteries without water are known as closed batteries; they can be more expensive, but last longer and don't require as much upkeep.

UPDATE AND INSPECT SMOKE AND GAS DETECTORS

This is an area a lot of people ignore or neglect, but they are actually two of the most important item to regularly check. Smoke detectors will often beep loudly if their batteries are low and you need to replace them right away since they are your first line of defense in a fire.

We'll talk more about fire safety in an RV later. It is just as important to replace LP and Carbon Monoxide gas detectors as necessary. You should also check propane lines regularly by spreading soapy water over them. If you notice any bubbles, you should immediately turn off the tanks and get the leaks repaired.

REPLACE OR CLEAN FILTERS

Filters that require cleaning and/or changing regularly are in the engines, generators, and air conditioners. Neglecting these can lead to clogging and problems. Often engine and generator filters are changed during a normal professional maintenance.

You won't need to change AC filters, but you'll need to clean them often. If you are using your AC often then you should check the filters at least once a week and clean them as needed.

MONITOR FLUID LEVELS

If the fluid levels get too low in an RV or if they get contaminated then your RV won't function properly. This is why you want to check all your fluids regularly. Doing this will help you avoid major mechanical problems with your RV.

SERVICING ENGINES AND GENERATORS

At least once a month you want to run the generator and engine to make sure they are lubricated, especially on a diesel run RV. Failing to do this will cause the internal parts to dry up and stop functioning.

These two items also require regular servicing by changing the oil and filters; checking and changing any fluids as necessary and doing anything else needed to keep them running well.

MAINTENANCE AND CLEANING OF HOLDING TANKS

Any RV has three tanks: black, gray and fresh. No matter how well maintained the rest of your unit, failing to properly care for these tanks will cause your RV to smell bad; making it uncomfortable to live in or travel with. Worse, failing to maintain these can lead to breakage and clogging; both of which are costing repairs. We'll discuss more about caring for and maintaining these tanks later.

SANITIZE AND CLEAN DRAINS, FAUCETS AND SHOWER HEADS

Over time debris can clog shower and sink drains. This is why you want to regularly clean drains as well as shower heads and faucets. Doing this can also keep your water flowing properly and avoid flooding.

When cleaning, make sure you don't use caustic materials or sharp tools to avoid damaging the drains or surrounding materials. It is best to use Baking Soda and clean the drain by hand.

MAINTAINING GOOD TIRE CARE

It is extremely important to take care of your RV tires, even if you aren't traveling often with the RV. We'll discuss specifics in a later chapter on maintenance and safety, but at the very least you need to be aware of four things:

1. Check regularly for damage.
2. Make sure there is adequate and equal air pressure.
3. All tires should be the same brand and size.

4. Use a gauge to ensure all tires have the right amount of air pressure.

CHECK APPLIANCES

You also want to regularly check your appliances and make sure they are working. Often times you may need to wash filters to get rid of dirt and dust; sometimes you'll also need to use an air compressor in order clean out clogged pipes. A few things to keep an eye on include the following:

- An ammonia odor from the refrigerator likely means you need to repair or replace it.
- Mildew smell from the AC means you need to clean the filters and vents.
- If you notice a gas smell, turn off the stove and open the windows. Leave the RV until you check the propane tanks for any leaks.

MAINTAIN DETAIL

Dirt and road grime can not only make your vehicle look bad, but they can also have a negative impact on the paint job, tires and undercarriage. Dust can also get inside and settle on upholstery, carpets and all interior areas; causing things to deteriorate over time. This is why you should detail the RV at least once or twice a year and thoroughly clean the interior every few days. We'll discuss cleaning in depth in the safety and maintenance section of this book.

LUBRICATE THE SEALS OF SLIDE OUTS

One of the biggest and most costly repairs to an RV is slide out repairs. To avoid this problem, the easiest thing you can do is keep the slide seals lubricated. When these seals dry out, they will start to stick, which can lead to a number of maintenance issues. This process only takes a few minutes and can save you a lot of money on repairs.

Doing these thirteen things consistently will keep your RV running well and safe to live in a while on the road. In order to maintain and protect your RV it is important to have a toolkit on hand, but with not much room you need to make the most out of the kit you have. Let's look at the ideal toolkit you should keep on hand.

Here are couple of You Tube videos on how to protect and maintain your investment.

Protection from winter and how to keep warm

https://www.youtube.com/watch?v=o5MBzWk9BAM

This next video is about a pre departure checklist

https://www.youtube.com/watch?v=mRIyY2XxzgA

THE IDEAL RV TOOLKIT

If you are going to live out of an RV or van, there are certain pieces of equipment you need to have in a toolkit so you can do basic repairs as well as be prepared for emergencies. The right tools will keep you safe while saving your money and allowing you to live more comfortably. At the least you toolkit needs to include the following:

- The right small tools.
- The right kind of air compressor.
- A reliable tire gauge.
- Two sets of wheel chocks.

Let's take a look at each of these areas in detail to make sure you have everything you need before you start living out of your RV full time.

THE RIGHT SMALL TOOLS

There are some basic small tools that you should always have on hand. Most all of these tools will fit into a small portable toolkit that is easy to fit in the small storage space of an RV. Depending on the vehicle you choose you'll need to consider a variety of types and sizes for certain tools such as wrenches so make sure you make the right choices. The following is a list of tools you should always have:

- Pliers
- Blade Fuses
- Protective gloves
- Tire-changing equipment
- Vise grips
- Wrenches
- Wire brush
- Box cutter
- Razor blades
- Pry bar
- Hammer
- Small saw
- Tube of silicone
- Hose clamps
- Screwdrivers
- Nails, screws, nuts, and bolts
- Adjustable wrench
- Bungee cords

- ☐ Small shovel
- ☐ Zip ties
- ☐ Rope
- ☐ Electrical tape
- ☐ Duct tape
- ☐ Tape measure
- ☐ Voltage meter
- ☐ Water pressure gauge
- ☐ Extra hoses for both water and sewer
- ☐ Bubble stuff to test propane lines

THE RIGHT KIND OF AIR COMPRESSOR

The most important thing when living an RV lifestyle is to know how to maintain and use tires. Proper care includes knowing how and when to inflate tires without causing damage. Most people new to RV living assume you can simply air up their tires at a gas station or truck stop. However, there are three things wrong with this way of thinking:

1. Air compressors at gas stations don't put enough air into RV tires to properly inflate them.

2. Truck stops may not always be available when you need them.
3. Public air pumps often contain water that can get into and ruin your tires.

This is why it is important to have your own air compressor unit on the RV and make sure it provides the proper psi. Having an air compressor is also a multi-use tool that you can use to inflate other items on your RV as well.

However, there are many types of air compressors on the market, and you want to make sure you are getting the right one for your needs. The right air compressor is one that is 150 pounds psi. This will give you enough strength to inflate tires; but it is still light, compact and easy to store.

A RELIABLE TIRE GAUGE

This is another important item you need to have if you are going to live in an RV. Buy a decent and reliable gauge, and make sure you regularly test it to ensure it is maintaining its accuracy. You can even choose to get a wireless system that gives you instant and accurate readings from inside your RV, so you will always know that your tires are properly inflated.

The air pressure in RV tires is a major safety issue that you shouldn't take for granted. If you are driving, you should check tire pressure on each tire several times a day. You definitely want to check them before heading out on the road to make sure it is safe to drive. If tires on an RV aren't equally inflated to the right levels, then you are at risk of a blowout; which can lead to a major accident.

I installed an automatic tire pressure monitoring system on my RV; I strongly suggest you do too. This is the best $500 investment you can ever do for your RV. This will give you a great piece of mind.

TWO SETS OF WHEEL CHOCKS

This is one of the least expensive, but most helpful items you can have on hand. Make sure you choose the appropriate size and weight for your RV. They are very helpful for use in unstable parking conditions. It is best to have two sets on hand in case of breakage. You should never park your RV unit without using wheel chocks to prevent wheels from rolling and causing an accident.

You may not think these items are that important at first, but once you have them, you'll be amazed at how often you use them. You may also find other items as you travel that you need to have on hand. Just make sure you keep your toolkit as well stocked and maintained as your actual RV, so you are ready for anything that comes your way.

Now that you are prepared for life in an RV let's start looking at getting some the basic utilities ready.

ADDITIONAL SAFETY FEATURES YOU CAN ADD

If you are buying a used RV, chances are it will not come with some of the modern safety features or driving aids. I have added a few must-have features onto my own RV, and I highly recommend you do too. Here is a list with an average cost to buy them.

Backup Camera System Average cost around $150-$200

Blind-Spot monitoring system. Average cost around $400, consider paying another $150 to have it installed.

A Birds-eye view look all around the RV with a separate monitor. This can set you back around $500-$700 depending on where you go to get this kit. But getting one that has night vision can be very helpful for night parking

TPS- Tire Pressure Monitoring system. This is an absolute must-have in my opinion. A good system can cost around $300 to buy and around $200 to install.

GPS System. If you are planning on using your phone as a GPS, think again, handling a big RV on a busy road is hard as it is, so go for a stand-alone GPS from Garmin or one that installs in the dash.

A smaller unit from Garmin that hangs from your windshield or sits on the dash can cost around $150. But one that goes inside your dash and doubles as radio, CD player and such, may cost you around $500.

Here is another You Tube video about how to install a back-up camera on your RV.

https://www.youtube.com/watch?v=jXSuu0poBn0

This next video is about proper towing safety with your RV.

https://www.youtube.com/watch?v=-DQ4lLPygoQ

Here are two videos about RV travel safety measures you can take.

https://www.youtube.com/watch?v=Pxkjv4Oeg6U

https://www.youtube.com/watch?v=rgfZ8q4VCXE

UTILITIES IN AN RV

Perhaps the first question you are asking yourself about living in an RV is how you will access your basic utilities. Especially if you plan to go off grid in an RV, then you won't be hooked up to the grid, and you'll still need to run the AC, bathe, book and use the toilet.

However, you are likely going to have no trouble doing these things in an RV since many of them are self-contained and have their own utilities and plumbing systems that can operate for a short period of time.

While the systems in RVs can vary, all units will at least have holding tanks, propane tanks, batteries and basic plumbing systems that allow you access to water, some level of power and basic bathroom facilities. Most RVs will also come with generators, solar panels and inverters to give you a variety of electricity levels. In general, the more utilities you have, the more comfortable you'll be when living in an RV.

Most RVs are more like an apartment on wheels with their own heating and air conditioning systems that are self-contained. The size and design of an RV will determine the number and type of utilities provided, and since you are often going to be stationary when living in your RV, you'll have several options for accessing utilities.

You can either connect to the utilities at campgrounds with hoses and electrical wires, or you can choose to use your own sources such as generators, inverters, batteries, solar panels and propane gas.

HOW THE PLUMBING WORKS

Most RV have plumbing systems similar to those found in traditional homes, but they are often made from thinner materials and function a bit differently, meaning they require a little extra care. RVs have built-in gray and black water tanks that hold waste in enclosed areas.

You start by filling your fresh water tank at home or in a campground, use the water as needed and then empty it as gray water. You attach a hose to the built-in tank and then release the liquids into a sewer outlet simply by pulling a handle.

UTILITY HOOKUPS

Most campgrounds will provide you with utilities that you can connect to your RV. If you choose to dry camp, this refers to a situation where no hookups are available, such as truck stops or BLM camping areas. The majority of places don't provide sewers but do provide you with "dump stations" where you can empty your tanks. These "dump stations" are also often available at rest areas and truck stops. However, some places will charge you to use "dump stations" at the cost of around $15.

A SELF CONTAINED UNIT

Since most RVs are a self-contained unit, they can often function without having to be hooked up to utilities. The tanks in an RV will hold fresh, gray and black water while propane will run refrigerators and stovetops; generators and inverters will provide electricity and batteries provide 12-volt service. This means you don't have to stay in a campground if you don't want to since you can use your own utilities on a short-term basis.

UTILITY SOURCES

Propane is a source that you may need to refill often since you'll use them regularly. You can fill them at campgrounds, truck stops, and gas companies. Currently, propane will run you about $3 a gallon, and a gallon will last about an hour.

Another option is batteries. There are two types to consider: coach and engine. A travel unit uses the batteries to run internal lighting and also energize the engine of a motorhome. You will need to maintain batteries and replace them from time to time, but without a battery, RVs can't function.

Another electricity option is solar panels. Some RVs will have these panels on their roofs that provide a small amount of electricity to the RV. These panels will often help run inverters which can power TV sets and some small appliances. This will often help you save money by eliminating the need for propane.

Generators are often a popular choice. You can find ones that run on propane, gasoline or diesel. These are a popular way to get electricity when you aren't hooked up to the electricity at a park.

Last is the inverters. The inverters get power from batteries, generators, a running engine or solar panels. These inverters produce energy for low-level appliances to save money on the cost of fuel for generators.

This is just the basics for utilities and electricity. Let's look a little closer at purifying and protecting your water as well as what you need to do to get communications while living in your RV.

PROTECTING AND PURIFYING WATER IN AN RV

The best way to assure you have safe drinking water while living on the road is to take the necessary steps to protect your water supply, so it stays clean and pure. When living in an RV or van, one of the most common ways people get sick is by drinking contaminated water, and the results can be bad. Let's look at how you can keep your water supply pure and clean so you can stay healthy when living on the road.

Those who stay at campgrounds and live on the road often don't realize that the water they are drinking in some places may not be safe. Even drinking from a running stream could mean you are ingesting bacteria, viruses, and parasites.

Some facilities that you stay at won't properly monitor their water supplies, and this can lead to health problems. There are a few steps you can take to protect yourself.

The first thing you need to do is to avoid the assumption that all water is safe since there is a big difference in purity, quality, and type of water depending on the place you are staying.

Even if water is safe to drink, the fact is that water with a different chemical structure from what we are used to or water that comes from a foreign source can cause us to become sick or make our immune systems weaker. Some common issues include rashes, diarrhea, constipation, and hives.

Before you connect your water hose in any new area, you are staying you want to turn on the main faucet and run water for a minute or two. Then put some water in a paper cup so you can smell it and look at the color before taking a small taste.

While this won't ensure the water is good it can give you a few signs that you should definitely avoid. If the water has a bad odor, is cloudy or brackish or has any odd or unusual coloration, then you should avoid drinking the water. It is important that you always carry a few water purification tablets with you in case you think a supply of water isn't safe or clean.

It is also important that you properly sanitize and maintain your water tanks. We will discuss this in a later chapter on maintenance and upkeep of your RV. Once contaminated water is in your tanks the residue will remain even after you empty them. By sanitizing your tank, you can ensure that all fluids in it will be safe.

It can also be a good idea to install a water filtration system in your RV. While nothing can actually give you one hundred percent protection, at least it will provide you with an extra level of safety.

There are two types of filtration systems you can consider. The first is a built-in system that filters only what you drink, and the other is a system that attaches to your hose and filters all water you use in your RV.

Using these steps can help you keep your water pure and clean. Doing this can ensure you stay healthy while living on the road. The other thing you need to consider is how to communicate while on the road.

COMMUNICATIONS ON THE ROAD

Once you decide to live out of an RV or van, one of the biggest questions you'll be faced with is what you are going to do about mail, phone, and internet. After all, you won't have a residency, and you won't be able to establish yourself with something like a bank. Thankfully there are a few easy solutions to this situation. Let's take a look at each one.

MAIL

The simple solution to this problem is to get a mailbox at a UPS Store. You can either choose to keep one at a base location that you will stop by every so often. Otherwise, you can change to a new UPS Store as you move. However, this still doesn't solve the issue of establishing residency in a state.

When it comes to establishing residency, the first thing you need to do is choose a state. Keep in mind that some states have a heavier tax burden than others, so this can be a big factor especially if you have the income to report.

Another thing you'll want to consider is the cost of vehicle insurance since it can vary between states. Lastly, you'll want to consider the factor of vehicle inspections. You don't want to travel back to your home state every year just to renew your vehicle registration. Based on all these factors the best states to choose include the following:

- Nevada
- South Dakota
- Texas
- Florida

All of these states don't have state income tax and make it fairly easy for you to become a resident. When it comes to insurance, the lowest rates are in South Dakota.

Once you choose a state, you need to get a residential address and start receiving mail. The easiest solution is to use the address of a family member or friend if they happen to live in one of these states. Another option is to use a mail-forwarder.

These companies allow you to set up a mailbox with them and then they will send it to an address you give them when you are ready. You can then receive this mail as a

General Delivery mail at a Post Office, or you can get a package sent to a UPS Store, or you can check-in at an RV campground and have your mail sent there.

TELEPHONE

This is another simple option since most people have cell phones today. However, there are a lot of plans to choose from. If you don't use the phone that often you may do fine with a pay-as-you-go plan. You really just need to consider coverage and cost to determine which cell phone plan is right for your needs.

INTERNET

While living on the road, there are four main ways that you can get internet access:

First, you can get free internet access at a number of places throughout the United States. The most obvious locations are libraries since they nearly always have free internet. In larger cities, you can go to a place such as Starbucks and find free internet.

Second, you can get the internet on your cell phone. Most contract cell phones allow you to use your cell phone as an internet browser for a small fee. However, you'll have to get used to using a small screen. But lately, I have seen where T-Mobile, AT&T and

Verizon, all three companies are offering unlimited internet for a flat fee. If you can subscribe to that plan.

Third, you can use a data air card on your laptop to get broadband. This gives you broadband internet speed in nearly every city no matter how big or small it is. However, with this option, you are often limited to how much you can use before fees get really high.

Fourth, you can get the internet by satellite. This means you'll need to have a satellite dish on your RV or van and pay a monthly fee. Sometimes you may not be able to afford this cost or have space in your living area for a satellite. You'll need to do your own research to find the best option for your needs.

BANKING

Banking on the road has become very easy thanks to debit cards and the internet. ATMs allow easy access to cash, and you can make electronic payments through the internet. The internet also allows you to view your account, transfer money and pay your bills.

Most of the time people don't even need to go to their bank branches anymore and even if you do, you can choose a bank that has branches throughout the country so you'll always be likely to find a bank.

TELEVISION

Lastly, you may want to have a television for entertainment. This can actually be easier than you may think. You can choose to buy an LCD television with an HD digital tuner built in. These are small and don't require a lot of energy. You can often mount them on a wall with a swing-away mount, so they aren't in the way.

However, you may need to buy an antenna to get better reception, and this won't be able to fit on all RV and vans. Now that you have all your utilities ready to go let's take a look at what you need to consider to actually enjoy your life on the road.

Here is a video about watching TV on the road.

https://www.youtube.com/watch?v=PrA_uTbXkt8

LIVING ON THE ROAD

Perhaps the most popular idea that draws people to living on the road is the idea that they can live cheap or even rent free. While you can choose to pay to camp at RV camps with amenities, the truth is that you can stay at many places throughout the country for free. Let's look at some of your options and how you can live rent-free.

It is important to note that when you choose to stay for free, you might find yourself parking in areas that may not be considered the safest. Therefore, you always want to place safety first when it comes to living and spending the night. There are plenty of free and cheap places where you can stay, but if a situation doesn't seem safe, it is always better to pay to stay somewhere safe. So always place your safety first.

WHERE TO STAY RENT FREE

BUSINESS LOTS

There are plenty of businesses that are RV and van friendly, some even have large spaces reserved for this purpose. A few will even have security on hand. Even if a business allows for RV or van parking it is always important that you do four things:

1. Ask permission to use the facilities.
2. Purchase something from the business.
3. Never fully set up camp.
4. Dump your tanks on the ground.

When you practice these four rules of good etiquette, you can ensure you as well as fellow travelers will always be able to stay in these places. Four major businesses that will often accept RV and van travelers include the following:

1. Wal-Mart
2. Camping World
3. Pilot/Flying J Truck Stops
4. Most truck stops

A lot of other big box stores will often allow you to park overnight as long as you get permission first and park away from the normal traffic flow.

SMALL TOWN VENUES

In smaller towns you'll be able to find free overnight parking at the following locations:

1. Fairgrounds
2. City parks
3. County parks

If you are going to park and sleep the night in a city the first thing you need to do is determine the attitude towards RV and van living. Most cities have laws against sleeping in a vehicle while others are quite tolerant and tend to ignore those who live out of their vehicles. Some cities will even have areas designated for those who want to live out of their vehicles.

The best way to find out is to simply contact the local police department and ask. Another option is to go to the local Wal-Mart and looks for signs stating "No Overnight Parking." Whether living in your vehicle is legal or illegal you should consider practicing stealth parking.

This is living in a way that allows you to blend in and not draw attention to yourself. If you are going to practice steal parking, there are a few general rules you need to follow.

If possible, you should have the newest vehicle you can and make sure it is plain, clean and neat. Try to avoid anything that will draw attention to your vehicle.

You also want to spend the minimum amount of time at an overnight location. Ideally; you should arrive at the last minute, go to sleep right away and leave as soon as you wake up in the morning. The longer you are at an overnight spot, the more likely you are to draw attention to yourself.

Another way to keep from drawing attention to yourself is to keep noise to a minimum. Step outside your vehicle and see if anything is making noise. Noise not only draws attention to you but can also irritate others trying to sleep in the area.

Lastly, make sure you don't always stay at the same place all the time. The more times you return to the same parking lot, the more likely you are to draw attention. Therefore, develop a few different places to sleep overnight if you plan to stay in a city for a while.

Stealth parking is often only good for overnight stays and not for long-term living situations. If you need to stay someplace for a few nights first consider looking into free campgrounds that offer you basic utility hookups.

FREE CAMPGROUNDS

Most aren't aware of the fact that there are a number of camping facilities throughout the United States that allow you to camp for free or a small donation and they still have utility hookups for you to use. These options are often a good choice since they are safe and better than parking someplace with no security.

DRY CAMPING

This is something you need to consider carefully before choosing to do. Some locations for dry camping are safe, but others may not be as safe. Dry camping is often done at government-run parks with no hookups. This would be Bureau of Land Management and Corps of Engineers facilities. Just be prepared that most of these places are located in desolate areas. Also, know that most of them don't have security available in the event you run into issues.

STAYING AT CASINOS

A lot of smaller casinos throughout the country will allow you to dry camp. A few will even have full hookup campsites with security. Anyone can park and stay at a casino as long as you ask permission first and you aren't required to gamble.

There is also another option if you want to stay at campgrounds and RV sites. Let's look at some ways you can stay at campgrounds for free or at least reduce the cost of your stay.

EXCHANGING WORK FOR LIVING

The easiest way to stay for free at a campground is to offer your labor. This is true at a lot of private campgrounds or RV parks. Often you will only be required to do minimal work part time and still have plenty of time for other activities. Some jobs you may be asked to perform include the following:

- ☐ Registering guests
- ☐ House Sitting
- ☐ Clerical duties

- ☐ Mowing lawns
- ☐ Cleaning bathrooms

If you don't want to work for free-living or don't need to, then there are plenty of other areas where you can find free RV living. An example of this is Slab City, a place where you can live free as long as you want and currently is home to about 200 people. All it takes it a little time and research to find a free place to stay.

VOLUNTEERING

Many state and national parks will allow you to apply to work as a volunteer. Often this work is seasonal, but if you go this route, you can often do part time volunteer work while getting a full hookup site at no charge. Many people choose to work in the North during the summer and then work in the South during the winter. Consider three benefits to choosing this route for free RV living:

1. You get to live in the middle of a beautiful park with wildlife, hiking trails, and fishing while paying nothing.

2. If you get to know other park workers that are local residents, you may be invited to their homes for parties and other social events.
3. Larger parks will also allow volunteers to enjoy a number of activities for free.

Each park offers different policies for volunteers, so it pays to do your homework and ask around before heading to a park.

FINDING FREE RENT DEALS

There are plenty of sources out to there to help you find free working/living opportunities. The Good Sam Club publishes a travel guide each year that can help you. Other options to finding free rent at campgrounds include the following three options:

1. Do internet research.
2. Visit local campgrounds and talk to the current hosts for advice.
3. Research various campgrounds to see if they offer free rent in exchange for work.

Rent free living in an RV or van is certainly an excellent option and you can often find a number of ways to stay free while on the road. However, if you find you need to stay at a campground that charges fees, there are a few things you can do to avoid those campgrounds that cost more than they are worth.

WHY SOME CHARGE MORE

When it comes to camping spots, there is often a wide range of prices. They can even go as high as several hundred a night. Some of the reasons for this difference in price include the following:

- Location
- Amenities
- Local tax structures
- Owner overhead
- Greed

Some places can deservedly charge more because they provide excellent accommodations with lots of amenities and ideal locations. Facilities that don't charge as much often aren't in the best of locations or have very little amenities.

What you need to do is learn the difference between the two types of parks and determine whether or not a park is worth the amount they are charging.

FINDING REASONABLY PRICED PARKS

The first thing you need to do is ask the right questions. Don't just ask for the price only. Rather go beyond this and ask the following questions to really find out how much a park is worth:

- Do they charge more for a pull through the site?
- Do they charge extra for amenities such as cable, Wi-Fi, sewer or 50 amp connections?
- Do they charge for using the showers?
- Do they charge more when a special event is occurring?
- Do they charge for campfire wood?
- Do they charge to use washers and dryers?

Getting answers to these questions can help you decide on the best place to stay. There is no reason to pay upwards of a hundred a night when you can stay at a similar park with the same amenities for under twenty dollars a night.

No matter where you choose to stay, it is important that you stay safe while living on the road.

Here is a cool video of a couple finding boondocking (Dry Camping) out on the road.

https://www.youtube.com/watch?v=Aw0cnJ8Xql4

SAFETY WHILE LIVING ON THE ROAD

One thing that many don't consider when it comes to living on the road is just how dangerous it can be. Before you start to live on the road it is important that you do everything you can to protect yourself as well as others while on the road.

While you won't be able to avoid all issues, with some planning and preparation you can reasonably deal with most of the problems that can happen. Consider just a few things that you may face while living on the road:

- Predators
- Drunk drivers
- Thieves
- Scammers
- Breakdowns

Let's take a look at what you can do to prepare and plan for these events.

DEFENSIVE DRIVING

It is important that you learn how to drive your home, this is especially true for the larger RVs. You also want to learn how you can defend yourself while driving. To do this, you need to do four steps:

1. Take an RV training course.
2. Practice as often as possible before going on the road.
3. Test drive your RV before moving on the road.
4. Follow all safe driving guidelines.

Most mishaps on the road can be avoided by driving the posted speed limit, using caution when entering or leaving highways, carefully pull into truck stops and fuel islands and avoid distractions while driving.

VEHICLE UPKEEP

While repairing and maintaining a large RV can be time-consuming and costly; it is also extremely important. This is why many RVs fall into disrepair. An RV or van that isn't kept up can present a hazard on the road. Take the time to learn how you can do minor repairs yourself and check your vehicle regularly for any issues so you can safely use your home on the road for years to come.

SAFE CAMPING TECHNIQUES

Never assumes that anyplace you stop is completely safe, even campgrounds. Gone are the days when you could stay overnight in a rest area or camp in an unsecured area without worrying about safety. You never know who may be parked beside you. For this reason, you need to do three main things:

1. Don't leave doors or windows open.
2. Don't allow strangers into your vehicle.
3. Don't leave your vehicle after dark.

You also want to carefully choose the site where you park. Look for hazards and not just suspicious people or vehicles. Also look for wasp's nests or other pest hazards. Something as simple as parking on a lot that isn't level can have serious issues with your camping.

As we discussed earlier, you also want to test the water before drinking it. When you stay on guard and use common sense, you will be able to protect yourself and others.

Once you've chosen a spot and settled in, you need to keep in mind that there is often only 3 inches of the wall protecting you in an RV or van. This means you should do six things to protect yourself and others.

1. Try to stay overnight in campgrounds or well-populated areas that are monitored.
2. Keep cash and valuables out of sight.
3. If you don't feel safe, drive away and find somewhere else to stay. p
4. If you hear something suspicious, don't go outside to investigate, rather call the campground manager or 911.
5. If you are going to have a gun on hand, make sure you have proper training in how to use it.
6. Keep windows covered so it can be difficult for people to see inside and know where you are.

PREPARE FOR ISSUES

One of the best ways to stay safe when living on the road is to prepare yourself for any issues that may come up while on the road. You can do this in three steps:

1. Do a system and mechanical check of your vehicle before you leave a location.
2. Carry the equipment we discussed earlier to help you be prepared for issues.
3. Always make sure you have a balanced road and properly inflated tires.

HAVE AN ESCAPE PLAN

A vehicle can often give a false sense of security since they look solid and safe. Remember that they aren't. Consider three facts when it comes to RVs.

- RVs collapse quickly in front-end accidents.
- RVs roll over easily due to their high centers of gravity.
- RVs can catch fire easily.

If any of these situations happened, would you know what to do? If you don't, you're not alone; most people don't know what to do. This is why you want to take the time to develop an escape plan in the event of the three incidents above so you'll always know what to do. You may even want to practice regularly.

To develop an escape plan you want to learn how to use your emergency exits. Make sure you know how to use exit windows and have a plan of action in place if you need to leave quickly. If there is a problem at the front of the RV, you need to instinctually leave through the rear window exit rather than try to leave through the front entry.

Depending on the unit you have you may even want to consider getting a folding escape ladder, so you don't have to jump out of your RV in an emergency. Perhaps the biggest emergency you can face in an RV is a fire. Let's look at how you can be prepared for this event.

FIRE SAFETY

When it comes to fire safety there are four points you need to keep in mind:

1. Understand what causes fires in RVs.
2. Inspect regularly for problems and deal with them.
3. Have protective equipment on board.
4. Learn what you need to do in the event of a fire in your RV.

Never assume you are safe from a fire hazard. Fires can happen at any time given the right circumstances and are often the main cause of loss of life and property for those living in an RV. First, let's consider what happens when a fire occurs in an RV.

Even larger RVs tend to only have about 400 square feet of living area, and in this space, there is a number of flammable materials that can quickly spread the fire. The facts show that a fire can grow in as little as 20 to 30 seconds in an RV. This is why you need to know about fire safety in an RV. It is also important to know about the common causes of RV fires so you can prevent them.

Nearly 6,000 fire a year occur in motor homes, campers and travel trailers. You can prevent some of these fires and others can occur with no warning. Let's look at some of the common causes of RV fires and how you can prevent them.

A lot of things in your RV function off propane: refrigerators, furnaces, ovens, and stoves. Propane is highly flammable and can easily catch fire. It typically catches fire when there is a leak in the appliance or gas line itself. You can address problems before they happen by regularly inspecting propane items. You can do this in two easy steps:

1. Brush the gas lines with soapy water and watch for bubbles. If you notice any leaks immediately close off the lines and get them repaired as soon as possible.
2. If you ever smell propane in your vehicle, then you should check to make sure all pilot lights are lit and make sure all appliances are turned off properly. Make sure you air out your RV before you relight the pilot lights. If this isn't the issue, then open all doors and windows, turn off the propane at the canister and contact a repair shop right away.

You should also have an updated gas leak detector in your vehicle. This will give you a loud warning signal if a gas leak occurs. If a fire starts, a smoke detector will also sound an alarm. The moment you hear an alarm you should evacuate right away and call 911.

Another common cause of fires in RV is a fuel or fluid leak in the engine. These are most common in diesel engines. To prevent these fires, you need to do three things:

1. Check the engine compartment regularly.
2. Have your engine professionally cleaned often.
3. Have a fire suppression system installed in your engine compartment.

A suppression system will activate when the engine overheats and quickly extinguish any fire.

Many don't realize that wheels, tires, and brakes on an RV can also lead to fires. The wheel bearings can potentially dry up, causing friction and as result fires. Keep wheel bearings lubricated to reduce the risk of fires.

Unmaintained tires can also lead to blowouts. This can lead to both accidents and/or flying debris that can catch fire. In the section on maintenance, we'll discuss how you can maintain your RV tires safely. But there are four main things you can do for your tires:

1. Make sure the tires aren't too old.
2. Regularly check air pressure.
3. Ensure all tires are the same size and brand.
4. Take the needed step to protect tire integrity.

Lastly, if you forget to release your brakes when driving the vehicle, the rubber can overheat and catch fire. You will often smell the hot rubber and have time to correct the mistake before a fire happens.

Another cause is faulty wiring in many of the electrical wires for appliances. As wires age, they become brittle and crack. This can start a fire. Often you will be able to smell a burning wire before it actually turns into flames.

However, regular inspection of wiring can prevent this risk. If you do smell a burning wire, then you should turn off the electricity and start looking into the cause of the problem so you can repair it.

Using the stove and oven for cooking in an RV can lead to fires, especially if the propane catches on fire. A spill or an accidental touch of a potholder to the flame could easily ignite a major fire. Rather you may want to consider using a microwave, crock pot, electric coffee pot and electric frying pan to avoid any issues with starting a fire due to cooking.

Lastly, you have to worry about highway accidents. Most of these are the results of four things:

1. Lack of proper driving skills.
2. Drunk or drugged drivers.
3. Poor road conditions.
4. Bad weather.

You can prevent these by improving your driving skills, traveling on better roads when possible, avoiding travel during weather problems if possible and keeping a keen eye out for the behavior of other drivers. Even doing these things won't completely eliminate your risk for highway accident.

If you find yourself in a situation that the vehicle is o fire you want to exit as soon as possible. If you can't exit through the front door, then you need to use special escape windows located in all RVs. Practice escaping until you are comfortable and can do so quickly.

Practicing these things can help you stay safe while living on the road. While safety is extremely important, you also want to do what you can to stay comfortable on the road. Let's take a look at how you can stay warm and cold while living on the road in a vehicle.

HEATING AND COOLING IN A VEHICLE

You will soon find that one of the negatives of living in a vehicle rather than a home is the fact that they get cold in the winter and hot in the summer. With little in the way of climate control in a vehicle, you need to do some preparation and planning in order to stay warm in the winter and cool in the summer.

The first thing you need to do is inspect the slide, windows and door seals on your RV to make sure you are ready for the winter.

Maintain and lubricate the rubber seals on the windows, doors, and slides regularly, so they don't become cracked and torn. If a seal becomes bad you should replace or repair it. A damaged seal will let air into your vehicle since the fit won't be perfect. Once you are done checking the seal you need to look for air leaks inside your vehicle.

If you find there are drafts from air leaks inside your RV, you can often fix these with a little rubber or some spray foam insulation. However, there are also some options you can do to keep yourself warm in the winter for the short term.

Obviously, the simplest solution is to simply choose a temperate climate to live in year-round or travel to better weather. There aren't many places with year-round temperate climates, so many who live out of their vehicles choose to be snowbirds.

These are people who move south in the winter and then north in the summer to avoid any extremes in temperature. If you don't want to drive these long distances, then you can consider going up in elevation during the summer and down in elevation during the winter.

Another priority you need to do is add insulation to your vehicle. This will help keep the heat outside in summer and the warm air inside in the winter. You need to insulate and stop air gaps; you can do this in a few ways.

REFLECTIX

Most heat gain and loss is through the windows of a vehicle. Therefore, your first priority should be to cover the windows; which also helps provide you with privacy. The first step is to tint the windows as dark as you can within the legal requirements of your state.

The second step is to cover the windows with Reflectix. This is basically two heavy sheets of aluminum foil over bubble wrap. Often you can simply apply it with pressure, but you can also use 2-sided Velcro tape to apply.

You also want to put up a curtain or blanket between the back of the vehicle and the driving area. The glass of the front windows will cause you to gain or lose a lot of heat. Hanging a blanket or curtain will help with both insulation and privacy. The heavier the curtain, the better your insulation.

You can even consider a two-layer option and combine it with Reflectix so you can reflect heat back into the living area while providing a vapor barrier so the front windows won't fog up; which is helpful if you plan to Stealth Park.

It is also important that you stop drafts. Moving air causes you to feel cooler than the actual temperature, so you'll want to close all air gaps you find; especially those around doors. The best way to do this is with weather-stripping and caulk.

In addition to insulating your vehicle, you can also manage the cold by properly layering warm clothes. Dressing warmly while in your vehicle can help you improve your comfort level. Consider the following tips to help you dress appropriately in the cold:

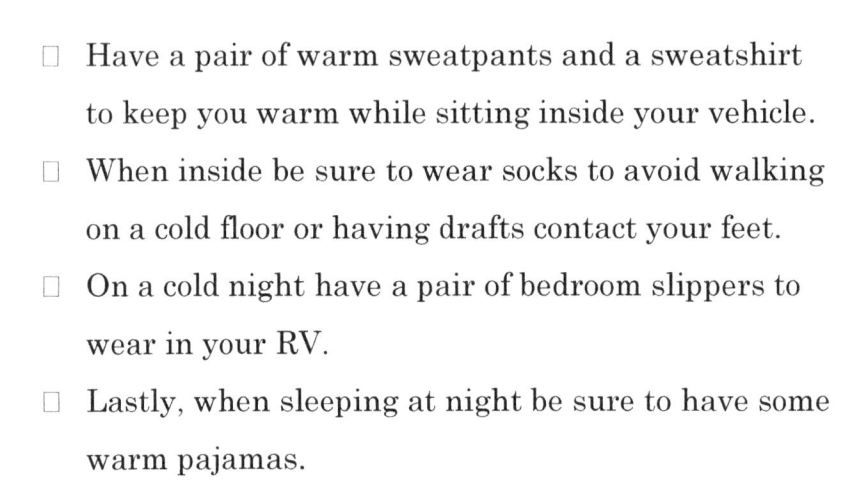

- Have a pair of warm sweatpants and a sweatshirt to keep you warm while sitting inside your vehicle.
- When inside be sure to wear socks to avoid walking on a cold floor or having drafts contact your feet.
- On a cold night have a pair of bedroom slippers to wear in your RV.
- Lastly, when sleeping at night be sure to have some warm pajamas.

For a cold night in a vehicle, a great option can be an electric blanket. An electric blanket on your bed at night will keep you comfortable while you sleep, even if temperatures aren't very high.

Perhaps the most important investment is the purchase of a good ceramic space heater. A space heater can bring the interior temperature of a vehicle up a few degrees. These are often cheap to operate and provide steady heat if you are going to be in your vehicle throughout the day. When choosing a space heater, look for one that meets the following requirements:

- Choose a space heater with small footprint since storage space is often a priority when living out of a vehicle.
- You should get a ceramic space heater since these have the best safety record than other types of space heaters.
- Look for a space heater with a built-in sensor to turn the heat off if it is knocked over to prevent a fire hazard.
- The space heater should have a multi-speed fan in order to adjust the amount of heat.
- Choose a space heater with a removable filter that you can clean and replace should it become clogged with dirt and dust.

If you plan to live anyplace with a cold climate for a couple of days or more you should properly prepare for the cold so you can live comfortably. In a later chapter, we'll look closer at how you can winterize your entire RV to be prepared for a long stay in cold climates.

The opposite is also true in the summer months when the temperature inside a vehicle that is sitting in the sun can rise quickly to unsafe levels. Take the necessary steps to maximize airflow to keep a comfortable temperature inside your vehicle and beat the summer heat. Let's look at the steps you need to take to stay cool when living from your vehicle in hot weather.

The first step in keeping your vehicle cool in the summer is to understand the basic rules of nature. Keep in mind five basic facts to help you learn how to cool your vehicle in the summer:

1. The night is always cooler than the day.
2. The sun rises in the east and sets in the west.
3. Shaded areas are cooler than direct sunlight.
4. Moving air cools you, while still air is hotter.
5. Hot air rises while cold air drops.

The first step is to utilize shade as much as possible. Shaded areas are often five degrees cooler than direct sunlight. This means you should look for shaded campsites. There are also other ways that you can create your own shade if needed.

The moment you set up your vehicle, make sure you open all window awnings. These awnings will shade your windows and cool the air around the vehicle exterior. You also want to position your vehicle, so the largest awning is on the east or west side of your vehicle depending on where you're most likely to spend time outside.

If you are going to be outside mostly in the morning, the awning should be on the east side, and if you are going to be outside mostly in the evening, then you want the awning facing west.

For added shade, consider stretching a tarp over your campsite. Tarps are a wonderful item that is cheap, easy to store in a vehicle and can dramatically cool temperatures in the summer.

If you don't have an awning or a tarp you can consider using a big beach umbrella. Sticking an umbrella in the ground will provide you with a little place of shade while you're outside your vehicle.

The second step you need to do is to create air circulation. Open all windows that are on the shady side of your vehicle and keep the windows on the sun side closed. This helps provide natural air circulation. You can also park your vehicle in a way that allows your ceiling fans to pull in cool air instead of hot air. It is also important to close the blinds on the sunny side to keep sunlight out of the vehicle.

A third option is to use your vehicles air conditioning. A lot of RVs today have a roof A/C unit. A little planning allows you to use the A/C for maximum effectiveness while reducing power consumption. With proper utilization of shade and screens, you may not even need to use the A/C. It is best to avoid turning on the A/C until the temperature is 75 or higher.

At this point be sure to close all windows and leave the ceiling fan on so it pulls out hot air at the ceiling; this will reduce the amount of load on the A/C. As the evening approaches the temperature cools so you can turn off your A/C and open on the windows to allow the cool evening air inside. Doing this can help reduce the energy usage of your A/C.

Proper planning means that for the fourth step you plan to do most of your cooking outside. This will help reduce the temperatures inside the vehicle. Consider three tips to help with this:

1. The best options are to use a grill, electric frying pan, electric broiler, crock pot or similar items.
2. Plan and buy your groceries so you can prepare everything outside.
3. Set up tables and chairs outside so you can cook and eat outdoors.

Lastly, consider planning your day to stay away from the vehicle. The hottest parts of the day are often eleven in the morning to about an hour before sunset. Plan your day, so you are gone during these hours. There are plenty of options for what you can do including the following:

- ☐ Shop
- ☐ See sites
- ☐ Fish
- ☐ Boat
- ☐ Swim
- ☐ Hike

Doing these things can help you stay warm and cool while living in your vehicle. The next thing you need to consider is cooking and eating while living on the road.

FOOD AND STAYING HEALTHY

Preparing and cooking meals in a vehicle while traveling on the road can be a difficult process. The difference is in your attitude and how easy you make it. Let's take a look at how you can prepare food while traveling.

Cooking and preparing food while on the road requires some adjustments, but once you make these changes, you will find it quite easy to prepare food and eat on the road. The galley of an RV is different from the cooking area in a home and in a van you won't even have a cooking area.

In addition, you'll often have to use propane for your cooking which requires you to adapt your timing since it burns hotter than electric. Even when you adapt to these differences, you will still have to prepare for some limitations in the types of meals you prepare.

STOCKING FOOD

Since you are going to have less room for food, it is important you shop carefully. Consider the following tips when considering what to buy and how to stock your food:

- ☐ A small freezer won't hold much-frozen food.
- ☐ Large bottles of milk or soda will take up space in a small refrigerator.
- ☐ Bulky vegetables won't often fit in refrigerator bins.
- ☐ Small items will often slide of shelves when the vehicle is moving.
- ☐ Too much fresh foods will spoil before they are eaten.
- ☐ Liquid items will often spill.

It is best to store food in plastic containers that are unbreakable and can be stacked easily. We'll discuss more about this when we discuss food storage and safety.

There are thirteen tips that can help make it easier for you to prepare and store food:

1. Use an under-the-cabinet coffee pot to heat water that can be used to make hot drinks, instant oatmeal, instant mashed potatoes, soups and other foods.
2. You can fill the coffee pot in the morning with hot water and then use it throughout the day, so you don't have to constantly use the generator.

3. Pull freezer items out in the morning, so they are thawed out by dinner time.
4. If you are going to drive for a long time, have a few frozen dinners on hand for a fast meal.
5. Keep a supply of dry nonfat milk on hand, so you always have milk available for when you need it.
6. Have meats on hand that can be thawed quickly when necessary.
7. Rather than baking; it is cheaper, cleaner and easier to buy baked goods.
8. Having fresh, frozen or canned fruits and vegetables will provide quick desserts and side dishes.
9. Save leftovers when possible for lunch.
10. Keep bread and cakes in the oven since it keeps them moist and reduces space.
11. Have a supply of crackers and cheese since they are good for snacks.
12. Avoid grills since they are bulky to store and difficult to clean.
13. Use paper plants and plastic utensils on travel days to eliminate cleanup and time.

FOOD PREPARATION

When it comes to preparing food on the road, there are a few things you can do to make it easier. First, you should consider a raw diet. With this, you won't have to cook, wash dishes, refrigerate or carry pans and pots. This is also an inexpensive and healthy alternative.

You can still eat a variety of fruits, vegetables, nuts, and seeds. In addition, some claim that cooking will kill the enzymes in food essential to good health.

Another option is to use basic and simple cooking. This option is good for those living in a van or smaller RV. With a small propane or butane stove and some safety measures, this can be a great option for those traveling in a van.

If you are living in a van, the biggest issue is a lack of refrigeration. This can often be simply solved by buying the perishable foods you need on the day you are going to cook and doing so in smaller portions that you don't have leftovers. It can be a good idea to travel with a cooler. It is best to buy a 5-day or extreme cooler. Another option is to get a small 12-volt compressor fridge.

Another thing to consider when it comes to storage space is your pots, pans, and utensils. For basic cooking, you won't need much. Often a single, three-quart pot can be used to cook canned foods and spaghetti while also being big enough to fry food as well.

Also, consider a griddle for when you need to cook for larger groups. When it comes to utensils you only need a spatula, can opener, knives, forks, spoons and a couple of plates and bowls.

COOKING METHODS ON THE ROAD

Now that we have the supplies and organization down let's consider how you can cook while traveling. An excellent option that works for most travelers is the pressure cooker. An oven is also a great option since it has multiple cooking options with low cost and size.

You basically need to look at your own circumstances and determine what cooking methods work for your living and eating needs. Now that we have the basics of cooking down let's look at how you can stay clean and healthy while living on the road.

Here is a video we like about how and what to keep in your refrigerator and on your cabinet, some great tips here.

https://www.youtube.com/watch?v=o-oFsyjyy0c

STAYING HEALTHY AND CLEAN

Another common question people have when considering living on the road is how to stay clean. In an RV this isn't too difficult since there is a fully self-contained system with running hot and cold water as well as bath facilities. However, in a van, it can be more difficult but not impossible.

Most of the time the main question is how do you shower? Although this brings up the definition of a shower. If you are talking about standing under hot water, the answer is different from those who simply want to have a clean body.

You can easily clean yourself by putting water in a basin with mild soap and then wash all of your body with a washcloth. Then you rinse with a soap-free washcloth.

Consider the following tips to help yourself stay clean while living on the road:

- Wash frequently - rather than getting one big shower you need to keep yourself clean throughout the day.
- Wash up at public restrooms - carry a washcloth in a Ziploc or use facial cleansing pads.
- Use portable diaper wipes to clean after you go to the bathroom.
- Carry a small bottle of alcohol antibacterial gel to clean when you don't have any visible dirt on your hands.
- Consider using an antibacterial soap such as Palmolive dish soap so you can double up your use.
- Make sure you have enough washcloths on hand to last at least 14 days since you may not do the laundry that often.
- For hard to reach places if you don't want to pack a large basin with you, then you can use a spray bottle to wet and rinse.
- If you want to shower consider using a solar water bag to get yourself some warm water.
- Always wash your feet separately to avoid fungus.

- Consider washing your hair in a public washroom. Or if this isn't possible, you can use a large basin or spray bottle. After wetting your hair, you can lather and then rinse with the basin or spray bottle. It can be a good idea to keep your hair cut short, so there is less to wash.

If you really need to shower, it isn't that hard to set up a shower; the main issue is having the room. Simply hook up a shower bag, stand in a large tub and open the spigot to shower. However, remember to conserve water. So you might want to wet down with a spray bottle, lather and then rinse with the shower bag.

Alternately, if you can't shower in your vehicle and have no place outside to set up a shower then you can consider some public locations that may offer shower facilities:

- YMCA
- College campuses
- Truck stops
- Gyms
- Public pools or beaches
- Laundromats

☐ RV parks

Living out of a vehicle on the road can make staying clean more difficult, but it's not impossible. With a little ingenuity and adjustment, you can stay clean and healthy while living on the road.

We've covered all of the basics you need to know and do on the road. However, living on the road means reducing your cost of living and getting the freedom to enjoy life. So let's take a moment to consider how you can find free and cheap entertainment while living on the road.

HEALTH CARE ON THE ROAD

If you are not old enough to be on Medicare then it may be little tricky to find a suitable health plan that can cover you while you are on the road. Since the fate of ACA (Affordable Care Act) is not looking good, but that was a great option for people like us who wanted coverage and didn't have to worry about finding a doctor or a hospital in or out of network. But I am sure our government will come up with something even better soon.

In the meantime, shop around for a policy that is not HMP but has PPO option where you can go to almost any doctor or hospital and not have to worry about being out of network.

Here is an excellent source for up-to-date information on health insurance on the road.

http://www.rverinsurance.com/

But if you are on Medicare, you are covered in all 50 states whether you have a Medicare Supplement Policy or not. One advice is to try not to change your Medicare plan to the Advantage plan as that plan is part of a network similar to HMO and you may have a hard time finding a doctor who is in your network.

FINDING ENTERTAINMENT & MAKING MONEY ON THE ROAD

Having the freedom of living on the road in an RV or van is a major advantage. While living on the road will save you a lot of money, you still need to learn to do things on a budget.

There are plenty of frugal ways that you can enjoy things such as nature, camping, social activities, hobbies, and entertainment. Consider some of the following tips to help you find fun and cheap entertainment while you travel and live in your vehicle.

FINDING CHEAP ENTERTAINMENT

Whenever you stop in a new city be sure to make your first visit to the Visitor's Center or the Chamber of Commerce. Here you can learn about the town, get an event schedule and learn about suggested things to see and do in the area.

You can often find a number of concerts, craft shows, and fairs in the area throughout the year. Most of these events are free and provide you with hours of fun things to do.

Depending on the city or town you visit you can consider getting around with a trolley or subway system. Often these only cost a couple of dollars for an all-day pass. This is easier than trying to get around in a car and often you can get a discount coupon at the visitor center.

If you are staying at a private campground, they will often have some form of live entertainment once a week. Most of the time this entertainment is free or only have a nominal fee.

Learn about the unique history of the local area by visiting local museums and parks. Most of these are free or very low in cost while providing you an interesting look at the history and culture of the area.

Another option is to visit State or National Historic Sites. Most of these have small museums for free or cheap. Here you can step back in time by wandering through historic buildings and sites. Along with this line, you can visit national parks and monuments. Most have museums and free Ranger-led tours or talks.

If you want to get outside, then consider hiking on any number of natural trails. BLM land and wildlife refuges have thousands of miles of trails to enjoy. Plus you may be able to see a number of native animal species as well. If you don't want to hike in nature, then consider a historic walking tour of cities. Most visitor centers will have maps that take you through the historic downtown of cities

In order to enjoy all the benefits of RV or van living then you need to practice good vehicle maintenance and upkeep. Let's look at how you can properly maintain an RV in order to have a safe and enjoyable life on the road.

MAKING MONEY WHILE YOU TRAVEL

Let me first break this to you; you won't be able to make a lot of money while you are on the road, unless you are a best-selling author or have a business that runs without you being there. Typically most people try to make a few extra bucks while on the road so it can cover the food cost or part of their fuel cost.

There are hundreds maybe thousands of passive income ideas out there, but it all depends on which ones are right for you. I am not an expert on this topic, but I can tell you, if you go on Amazon and type "Free eBooks on Passive income," you will see a list of over 50 FREE books that you can download and read. Once you read a few of them, you will get some great ideas and see which ideas match with your skills.

I am an accountant by profession, though retired, I found out I could offer my services on several outsourcing platforms like:

www.Fiverr.com

www.Guru.com

www.Upwork.com

All of this platforms offer the flexibility of working on your terms with whatever skills you have to offer. The skills could range from

- ✓ Bookkeeping
- ✓ Accounting
- ✓ Editing
- ✓ Graphics design
- ✓ Proofreading
- ✓ Various writing jobs

- ✓ Video, picture or even music editing
- ✓ Various programming
- ✓ Business advice
- ✓ Translation
- ✓ Digital or Social media marketing

And much more

Here is a very popular video about 6 ways you can make great money while RVing.

https://www.youtube.com/watch?v=o-oFsyjyy0c

RV MAINTENANCE AND UPKEEP

BEFORE YOU HIT THE ROAD
RV Maintenance Checklist

Appliances
- Refrigerator
- Inspect door seals
- Inspect burner flame
- Clean thermocouple tip
- Clean area behind refrigerator
- Furnace
- Check blower
- Check combustion chamber
- Check control compartment
- Inspect gas line
- Air conditioning unit
- Clean air filters
- Clean condensing unit
- Check voltage
- Hot water heater
- Flush every 6 months
- Clean burner tube
- Inspect sacrificial electrode
- Stove
- Make sure it produces blue flames
- Clear vents of animal nests and debris

Walkaround
- Inspect roof/body for cracks
- Check all lights and turn signals
- Check gas levels in propane tanks
- Charged fire extinguisher
- Test smoke detectors
- Test carbon monoxide detectors

General Maintenance
Check:
- Engine oil
- Transmission oil
- Tire pressure
- Tire wear
- Battery
- Brake fluid
- Power steering fluid
- Engine belts
- Engine coolant
- Windshield washer fluid

Plumbing
- Check that water pump flows well
- Flush waste tanks
- Inspect valves and water pump for leaks
- Inspect connection dump hose and fittings
- Sanitize water system

WINTERIZING YOUR RV

If you plan to spend the winter in a cold environment while living in an RV, you will need to make sure it is properly winterized. Winterizing your RV isn't all that difficult, but you will need to consider many facets.

While the water system obviously needs to be winterized, there are other parts of the chassis that need your equal attention. You also need to prepare the interior, the propane system, and the refrigerator before your RV is properly winterized. Anyone can winterize an RV, and we are going to make the process easy for you.

WINTERIZING THE WATER SYSTEM

Winterizing an RV water system can be done in one of two ways: using a special RV antifreeze and emptying the water system. In fact, a combination of both can be the best method.

RV antifreeze is a special solution that is semi-edible. However, this doesn't mean you should drink it; but the small amounts left in the system won't harm you. To use the antifreeze method you need to fill the fresh water tank with ½ water and ½ antifreeze so the onboard pump can pick it up and distribute it to all parts of the water system. Run the pump farthest from the water valve until you see the pink color coming from the faucet. Open both hot and cold lines, so both are filled with the solution.

Once the farthest outlet is producing antifreeze solution, shut it off and go to the next farthest; again running both hot and cold. Continue this process until all outlets are producing antifreeze solution. Make sure you don't forget any such as outside spigots, ice makers, hot water dispensers, water filters, etc. Once you are done, you want to drain the hot water tank.

For larger sized RVs this can be a difficult task that requires a lot of antifreeze. On the other hand, you can blow the lines empty of water. Purchase a fitting that you can put on the RV where the pressurized water normally goes and then use an airline fitting normally used to fill the tires.

You will need an air compressor for this. Once the air compressor is attached open the petcock on the hot water tank and drain it. Once you are only getting air, close the petcock and go to each water outlet. Make sure you empty both hot and cold lines. Once you are done, blow the water heater to make sure no water has drained in in the process.

WINTERIZING THE CHASSIS

There are two important things you need to do to winterize the chassis of your RV. First, check the exterior for cracked caulking and replace as needed. Also look for any exterior damage that could cause rain or snow to get into the RV.

You should also cover vents, awnings, and cavities if possible. If you can't cover them, then at least screen them. Otherwise, bees and other insects will nest in them.

WINTERIZING THE INTERIOR

Make sure no rodents or insects can access the interior. Seal all openings. Have window shades prepared to cover and prevent UV light from entering and degrading the upholstery while also helping to keep hot air inside the RV.

Here is a great video about how to winterize your RV the proper way.

https://www.youtube.com/watch?v=8Bo1VPGGiFo

Another thing you need to consider with your RV is to maintain and safely use your RV tires.

RV TIRE SAFETY AND MAINTENANCE

When it comes to RV tires; there is a lot to know about maintaining and safely using them. This is especially important since you don't want to make a mistake that could cost lives. Consider the following eight tips to help you:

1. Try to always park your RV on wood, concrete or gravel.
2. If you are going to be in one spot for awhile consider covering your tires to prevent dry rot.
3. Before, during and after driving your RV, you should use an accurate tire gauge to check air pressure. All the tires shoulder be equally inflated, too much pressure can lead to a blowout while driving.

4. Make sure you have tires that are rated properly to carry the weight of your RV.
5. Wash your tires regularly to prevent dirt and debris from building up in the treads.
6. If you have extensions on dual rear tires, then look for leakage and replace as needed.
7. Never put your RV up on jacks as this can cause damage to the structure of the RV.
8. Your tires can overheat in hot weather and expand before blowing out, so when traveling in hot weather try to drive only in the early morning and evening hours. If you need to travel during the day stop regularly to give the tires time to cool off and if needed hose them off with cold water.

Here is a great video on proper tire care and lots of good safety tips here.
https://www.youtube.com/watch?v=OzczHjvnXBo

Another area of your RV that requires attention for your health and safety is the dumping and deep cleaning of the sewer tank. Let's take a look at this process next.

DUMPING AND CLEANING THE SEWER TANK

Knowing how to care for and clean your black water tank is very important. It isn't that difficult to do and doesn't take very long, but it will keep your RV smelling good while ensuring your plumbing system functions properly.

Let's look at the simple four-step process you need to do when dumping and cleaning your black water tank.

PERSONAL PROTECTION

Since what comes out of the sewer hose is toxic it is important that you protect yourself and your clothing. This means wearing things such as rubber gloves, shoe covers, and protective glasses.

You should also have liquid soap and paper towels available to wash your hands at an outside faucet once you are done before going back into your RV.

EMPTYING THE TANKS

Once you are properly protected, you are ready to empty the tanks. Park your RV beside a sewer outlet. You will find these at campsites or dumping stations. At a dump station, you will connect the sewer hose to your RV and place the other end in the sewer opening. If you have a full hookup campsite, your hose will be connected to a sewer outlet.

During camping, you should have your waste water tank valve closed and your gray water valve open. Before dumping, you want to close the gray water valve and allow it to fill partly with soapy water. Don't wait to dump your tanks when they are full because the weight can damage or break your tanks.

To dump your tanks, you want to first open the black water valve. Once the waste is out of the tank you should fill the toilet with fresh water and then dump the tanks again. You should do this as often as needed to dump clear water. Once you have done this, you can open the gray water valve and allow the contents to be emptied into the sewer. This helps to clean the inside of the sewer hose and prevent the matter from sticking.

If you are going to continue camping, you can close the black water valve and add a gallon of water as well as some Spic N Span to the tank. If you are going to get on the road, then you should close both valves and put an enzyme clears in about one gallon of water in the sewer tank.

As you drive the mixture will move around and eat away at the hardened material to disinfect the tank and prevent clogs. It will also help eliminate odors that can make it difficult to live in your RV.

DEEP CLEANING

Some people think you only need to empty the sewer tanks in order to keep them clean, but you need to deep clean them for proper maintenance. You will need to dump every few days and deep clean at least once a week if you're using your RV for living purposes.

To deep clean, you want to follow the above steps for dumping your tank, but before opening the gray water valve you will do the following six steps:

1. Completely drain the waste water tank.

2. Fill the tank ¾ full with fresh water and two cups of bleach.
3. Allow the mixture to sit for 10 minutes, no longer.
4. Drain the tank.
5. Fill the tank again with ¾ fresh water.
6. Continue to drain and fill the tank until you see no debris in the clear hose connector and there is no bleach smell. You don't want to leave any bleach behind in the plumbing system since this can damage it.

After these six steps, you will need to pressure wash the inside of your sewer tank. To do this, you need to backwash the tanks; most RVs have these units built into the system. If you have one on your RV, you can follow the manufacturer's maintenance book on how to use it. If you don't have a built-in unit, then you will need to buy a wand that is made specifically for RV tank pressure cleaning.

With either method you want to backwash after dumping your sewer tank, but before you dump your gray water tank. If you are using a wand, it is a seven-step process:

1. Attach a green garden hose to the water spigot at your campsite.
2. Connect the backwash want to the hose.
3. Pull the wand and hose through a window or door into the bathroom.
4. Open the toilet flapper.
5. Put the wand down the opening.
6. Have someone outside turn on the water.
7. Move the wand back and forth around the tank until all of the waste has been cleared.

It is best to buy a clear sewer hose adapter in order to see when the hose runoff is free of debris. This will help you know your tank is completely clean.

ENZYME TREATMENTS

After dumping and deep cleaning the tank, you want to treat it immediately with a biologically friendly enzyme cleaner. You don't need to add this product every time you dump your tanks, but doing this occasionally will make it easier for you to do future cleanings and keep your tank from smelling.

These treatments are easy to use. Simply add a packet to your tank and add a gallon of water. The enzymes will eat away at sludge so it will easily flow through the plumbing system.

Following the above guidelines will keep your waste water tank clean, sanitized and smelling good. With regular cleaning and dumping of your tanks, you can't enjoy living in a safe RV. It is just as important to clean and sanitize the rest of your RV.

Here is a video that shows you how to dump and clean your black tank.

https://www.youtube.com/watch?v=I6sv4d3PsTo

CLEANING AND SANITIZING YOUR RV

Just as you would with a home, cleaning and sanitizing the living space of an RV is important for your overall comfort and health. In addition, it maintains the value of your RV should you decide to get out of the lifestyle and need to sell your RV. Cleaning and sanitizing your RV is a part of properly maintaining your RV. Let's look at how you can properly clean all the areas of your RV.

DUSTING AND VACUUMING

There are three items you need to use in order to effectively reduce dust in your RV:

1. Shop-Vac and attachments
2. Small hand vac
3. Long handled duster

Make sure you dust all areas including floors, windows, curtains, blinds, dashboards, upholstery, counters and inside drawers and cabinets. After vacuuming, wipe down the counters and exterior cabinets with ammonia water or Windex so they will be safe for food preparation.

WINDOWS, MIRRORS AND WINDOW TREATMENTS

If windows aren't covered with a solar film, then you can simply clean them with Windex. If your windows are covered with a solar film then you should follow your manufacturer's directions since certain cleaning products can damage them.

Make sure both sides of all windows are cleaned. Clean mirrors as you normally would in a home. Vacuum any valances as you would upholstery.

DASHBOARDS AND UPHOLSTERY

Once you have vacuumed the dash thoroughly you should clean all surfaces with vinyl or leather protector; be sure to clean the steering wheel and foot pedals. For leather furniture, you can use the same cleaner after wiping it down with a damp cloth. For fabric furniture, you want to vacuum well and then spray with Febreze or another refresher. It can be a good idea to have them professionally steam cleaned once a year.

CLEANING THE TOILET

To clean the toilet, you want to use products that are specifically designed to clean and disinfect without damaging. Doing anything else can lead to problems that can be expensive to deal with. You should never clean with brushes, non-disposable rags or rags with chemical residues from other jobs.

You want to clean the toilet at least once a week if you are going to be living out of your RV. To clean you should use disposable paper towels, water and a disinfecting pine-based cleaner like Pine Sol. Clean with a seven-step process:

1. Add water to the toilet bowl.
2. Pour cleaner into it.
3. Use paper towels to wipe down and disinfect the bowl and upper rim.
4. Clean under the rim as well.
5. Partially open the flapper and wipe it thoroughly.
6. Empty the contents.
7. Fill the bowl halfway with water and flush.

Check to make sure the bowl is completely clear of residue. If there is anything left then repeat the process. After the bowl is completely clean then you need to do six more steps:

1. Add some water and cleaner again.
2. Use the paper towels and contents to wipe the tops and bottoms of the seat as well as the sides and back.

3. Flush the toilet and add more water.
4. Use clean towels to wipe down what you just cleaned to get rid of sticky residue.
5. Spray the toilet with Lysol.
6. Dry the exterior of the toilet and you are done.

CLEANING THE BATHROOM

Depending on the size of your RV you may also have a shower stall and tub made from heavy plastic materials to clean as well. These can scratch easily, which leads to dirt buildup that ruins them. This can easily happen if you use the wrong cleaning products.

There are two ideal ways to clean the rest of your bathroom:

1. Wipe it down with a dry towel or squeegee after each shower and use Windex with Ammonia to clean metal and glass areas.
2. Spray with a product such as Clean Shower after each use.

For all other bathroom areas it is a three-step cleaning process:

1. Spray and wipe glass, mirrors, counters, sinks and exterior cabinets with Windex with Ammonia and paper towels.
2. Spray sinks, toilets, and counters with Lysol.
3. Mop or wipe down the floor with either ammonia products or a pine based deodorizing cleaner.

CLEANING THE FLOORS

The last part of the cleaning process is to do the floors. This can be a hard area to keep clean, but you can make it easier by doing the following:

- Vinyl, ceramic or tile floors can be cleaned with ammonia or ammonia and water.
- For laminate floors, you can dry mop first and then mist or mop with a mixture of vinegar and water with a microfiber floor mop.
- For carpets, you may want to consider protecting them with clear plastic runners and have them professionally steam cleaned on occasion.
- You can also use washable throw rugs while sweeping, vacuuming and laundering as needed.

Taking the time to clean and sanitize your RV will make it livable and safe for you. Once everything is cleaned you need to make sure you properly pack everything you need before heading out on the road.

PROPER LOADING AND PACKING

Properly loading and packing your RV is important for both comfort and safety. An RV is the same as any vehicle that needs to be well balanced in order to safely drive on highways and roads. Unbalanced loads won't drive well on slippery roads. Also, packing poorly can mean you miss packing important and necessary items you need before you reach your next destination.

THE IMPORTANCE OF PACKING AND LOADING PROPERLY

There are two main reasons why you want to make sure your RV is properly packed and loaded before you start driving down the road:

1. An unbalanced RV is dangerous and awkward to drive.
2. An improperly packed RV can be miserable to live in.

HOW TO BALANCE A LOAD

When loading your RV, the key is to keep the unit bottom heavy and make sure the items you pack are accurately distributed over the axles. The basics of this involve a five-step process:

1. Check the vehicle manual to see how much weight each axle can carry.
2. Weigh the RV when empty at a certified truck stop scale.
3. Pack your RV and place heavier items low and spread evenly along the entire length.
4. Weigh the RV again.
5. Make any needed adjustments.

The heaviest items are the appliances, slide rooms, engine, generator and water tanks. By weighing the RV, you will know which axles are already carrying the most weight. This information will tell you where to pack the lightest and heaviest. You also want to pack light items high and heavy items low. If you do this, your RV is less likely to roll over since you can have better control when driving.

TIPS FOR PACKING

If you are choosing to live out of a vehicle, then chances are you are already living a minimalist lifestyle, but if not you'll need to start. It is best to limit your choices to small items and those that perform double duty. Consider the basics that all RVs should have to live well on the road:

- A crock pot
- Electric frying pan
- Can opener
- Ceramic heater
- Cell phone
- GPS
- Clear, lidded and stackable plastic containers
- Multiple use items
- Multi-use clothing items for all seasons
- Food for a few days
- List of important contacts
- A toolkit
- Bad weather gear
- First aid kit
- Prescriptions and medications

In addition to these, you may have specific items that you need. No matter what you pack, it is important that you locate your items in the right places. Heavier and bigger items need to be packed low, but you also want to packs items, so they are easily accessed.

Perhaps the most important thing is to make sure you are packing the right foods while organizing and storing them properly. This can ensure your food stays safe, protects against insects and pets, avoid spillage and makes food easy to access. When choosing the food you want to choose food that travels well, tastes good, stores easily and isn't prone to spoilage.

RV FOOD STORAGE

As long as you have hot water on hand, you can easily mix powdered or dry foods such as:

- Dry soup mixes
- Instant oatmeal
- Instant potatoes
- Teas
- Instant coffee
- Hot chocolate

- ☐ Nonfat dry milk

While canned foods store well and have a long shelf life, they are also heavy and bulky. For this reason, you need to limit your canned items to only about a dozen or so. Stick to the basics such as the following:

- ☐ Baked beans
- ☐ Potatoes
- ☐ Fruits
- ☐ Vegetables

Group your canned goods in baskets so they won't slide around and you can easily access them.

Since you'll be making simpler meals, you will want to limit yourself to only the basic condiments such as:

- ☐ Mustard
- ☐ Ketchup
- ☐ Mayonnaise
- ☐ Lemon juice
- ☐ Salt
- ☐ Pepper
- ☐ Vinegar

- ☐ Sugar

Packaged snacks should be kept to a minimum since they take up a lot of storage space and can also be unhealthy for you. Choose to keep healthy snacks on hands such as the following:

- ☐ Popcorn
- ☐ Pretzels
- ☐ Vegetables
- ☐ Fruits
- ☐ Crackers
- ☐ Cheese
- ☐ Peanut butter

PROTECTING YOUR FOOD

Since RVs aren't as solid as homes, it is easier for vermin and animals to get into your food. There are three things you can do to keep pests and vermin away from your food:

1. Hiding ant and roach traps in closets.
2. Spraying RV tires, hoses and front panels with Pam.
3. Making sure RV screens have no holes.

When it comes to storing your food, you may be tempted to keep them in their original boxes. However, once you open them, you should transfer the contents to clear plastic, lidded and stackable containers that are airtight when sealed. Doing this will protect things from mildew, water damage, bugs, and vermin; keep food fresh and allow you to see contents so you can access them easily.

Many items are often packed in glass containers. It is best to either transfer these foods to plastic containers or buy in plastic if possible. If you need to buy something in the glass, then place them in a plastic basket and pack them as close together as possible. Store glass items on lower shelves or slide out pantries to avoid issues with weight distribution.

When storing food in the refrigerator be sure to use the following tips:

- Pack refrigerated foods as tight as possible.
- Smell milk for spoilage before drinking or stick with dry milk.
- Keep leftovers for as short a time as possible.

- Have a thermometer to make sure the refrigerator is cold enough to protect food.
- Make ice cubes at least once a week and store them in Ziploc bags.
- Make sure the refrigerator door is always closed and locked.
- Make sure your RV is level whenever you park so the refrigerator will keep working.
- Change the refrigerator settings to account for external temperature differences.
- Regularly defrost the freezer.

There is quite a bit of information, but by following all of these tips, you can have a safe and enjoyable life on the road in an RV or van.

LAST WORDS

I want to say THANK YOU for purchasing and reading this book. I really hope you got a lot out of it!

Can I ask you for a quick favor though?

If you enjoyed this book, I would really appreciate it if you could leave me a Review on Amazon.

I LOVE getting feedback from my wonderful readers, and reviews on Amazon really do make the difference. I read all of my reviews and would love to hear your thoughts.

Thank you so much!!

HELPFUL LINKS & RESOURCES

Best RV forums where you can find out about the latest trends, news and ask questions on any RV related topics.

https://www.tripsavvy.com/best-rv-forums-to-join-2912440

http://www.rvforum.net/joomla/index.php?option=com_content&view=category&layout=blog&id=123&Itemid=104

For RV Buying

www.eBay.com

www.Craigslist.com

www.RVTraders.com

www.CampingWorld.com/RVSales

For RV Price Checking

http://www.nadaguides.com/RVs

https://rvshare.com/blog/rv-values/

https://www.pplmotorhomes.com/kelley-blue-book-rv

Special Driver's License Requirements (If any)

https://www.outdoorsy.com/blog/guide-rv-drivers-licenses-requirements

To learn more about additional RV safety features, you can add to your rig visit here

http://www.livingthervdream.com/RV-safety.html

To find Free Campground in the US, visit these sites

https://ourroaminghearts.com/best-free-camping-sites-usa/

https://www.campendium.com/free-camping

https://www.freshoffthegrid.com/how-to-find-free-camping-usa-canada/

7 Best Smartphone Apps for RV owners (Some are free some are not)

https://www.tripsavvy.com/best-smartphone-apps-for-rv-travel-2912549

Finding Mechanics and Repair Shop while on the road

Try RV forum sites and post or search for mechanics in your immediate area

https://www.rvrepairclub.com/articles/all/

https://www.tripsavvy.com/best-rv-forums-to-join-2912440

For any DIY minor repair, I always find YouTube to be very helpful, so go there and learn how to do many minor repairs all by yourself.

www.YouTube.com

Health Insurance on the Road

http://www.rverinsurance.com/

Making a Side Income while on the road, for best ideas, go to Amazon and type "Free eBooks on Passive Income."

You can also check out these sites and see which of the skills matches with yours.

www.Fiverr.com

www.Guru.com

www.Upwork.com

Made in the USA
Las Vegas, NV
21 February 2023

67879827R00089